The Journey to Courage:

A Memoir

Volume I

By Christine Nathan

The town of Coniston is fictional,
although it represents a real place.
Some names have been changed also,
to protect privacy.

Edition © Christine Nathan 2021

A catalogue record for this book is available from the National Library of New Zealand.

ISBN 978-0-473-57563-2

Cover photos and artwork: Dreamstime and Bliss Design

Published by Christine Nathan

To my wonderful sons –Joshua and Eli, who reluctantly journeyed with me into the unknown and yet still accept and value me today. You grew into loving, generous, accommodating, family men of integrity and understanding.

I have appreciated your input, forgiveness and honest processing over the years as we recalled the incredible and sometimes tough journey that God led us on. I didn't always get it right but along the way we all discovered how tenderly God guides, provides and protects those who surrender their lives to Him.

You and your precious families are a source of constant delight, providing me with comfort, a sense of belonging and a safe warm place that fills my heart with gratitude and my soul with a deep sense of security.

To Vimbayi and Kay for your constant support and encouragement to write this incredible story for our family and future generations.

To Elisha, Raphael, Naniso Zoe and Kaleb – my precious grandchildren who are so much fun and a source of constant delight and love. I adore you all.

In writing my memoirs I trust that my children, grandchildren and future generations can learn from my mistakes as well as glean deep truths from the things that did go well along the way!

Thank you God for the abundance of a life spent following you.

Contents

The Road Not Taken

ROBERT FROST, 1916

Two roads diverged in a yellow wood
And sorry I could not travel both
And be one traveler, long I stood,
And looked down one as far as I could
To where it bent in the undergrowth;

Then too the other, just as fair,
And having perhaps the better claim,
Because it was grassy and wanted wear,
Though as for that the passing there
Had worn them really about the same,

And both that morning equally lay
In leaves no step had trodden black.
Oh, I kept the first for another day!
Yet knowing how way leads on to way,
I doubted if I should ever come back.

I shall be telling this with a sigh,
Somewhere ages and ages hence:
Two roads diverged in a wood, and I –
I took the one less traveled by,
And that has made all the difference.

Foreword

This book is not only a 'good read' but details a journey just as the title says 'Toward Courage….' Christine Nathan displays enormous amounts of raw courage on her journey and as you will see, there is layer after layer of courage, determination, faith, fortitude and strength that formed in her life, many of those qualities through the difficult situations she found herself in.

Today Christine Nathan is an amazingly whole woman who has allowed God to heal her over and over again, in spite of circumstances that would totally crush other individuals. Her relationship with God continues to grow and she exudes warmth, compassion and love in all her interactions.

As you journey with her through this book and through her life, you will be inspired and challenged. Within these pages you will find God's ways coming to the fore: forgiveness, love, compassion and faith. Herein are answers for any who are seeking healing in and for their own journey. You will laugh, cry and gasp as you travel through the chapters of this amazing book 'Journey Toward Courage' and as you do, our desire and prayer for you is that the same courage Christine has found and still living, will be within your grasp also.

Colleen Doyle

'GO' Ministries International

New Zealand

CHAPTER ONE

What a Wonderful World

1990

Selling up your home and belongings isn't an easy thing to do, especially when you are a single mother taking your two sons away from everything and everyone familiar to them in New Zealand and heading into the vast unknown continent of Africa.

What a life changer for a thirty-seven year old mother of sons Joshua, 16, and Eli, 10! I wanted to get the most out of the expensive flights, so I asked the travel agent if there were alternatives to the direct Auckland to Capetown flight she had booked for us. I hoped that we could see more of the world along the way. She suggested that for a slight increase in cost we could fly to Sydney, then London, with a quick stopover in Nairobi, Kenya, before heading to our final destination which was Capetown, South Africa.

These major cities were just names I had read about in National Geographic magazines or heard about on the news. But, because I was not sure I would ever get an opportunity to travel to different continents again, I was determined to see as many countries as possible along the way. After all, this trip was being paid for by the sale of our home.

Once we landed in Sydney, Eli would be leaving us to catch connecting flights to Zimbabwe where he would spend several weeks with his father, Solomon. Solomon and I had met in New Zealand when he was completing an engineering degree.

We had a relationship for a few years and then we separated when I was pregnant with Eli. Solomon moved back to Zimbabwe to establish a business when Eli was still a baby. Over the years, Eli had occasionally spoken with his father on the phone and when Solomon heard we were moving to South Africa, he invited Eli to spend time with his family. Since Eli was keen, I agreed. Eli would fly to Capetown after his family visit to meet up with Josh and me. As we left New Zealand, I became increasingly nervous about Eli traveling alone on such a huge journey, but I reassured myself that at least we would have some family time together when we landed in Sydney. I could encourage him and give him plenty of hugs before he began his long journey. To my shock, as soon as we landed and cleared customs, a staff member was waiting and whisked him away to catch his first flight. I began to panic, as it all felt too rushed and we hadn't even said a proper goodbye. All I could do was pray and ask God to take care of him. Having never travelled outside of New Zealand, I had no understanding of the enormous culture shock he was about to experience. He was going to a totally different culture, with strange food, unfamiliar people, and an unknown language being spoken all around him.

Meanwhile, Josh and I headed for the arrivals lounge where we waited for Jenny and Ian, friends who had lived near us in Coniston before recently moving to Sydney. They had prepared their garage as our 'home' for the ten days we would be in Sydney.

After an hour of waiting, I was relieved to see Jenny. She helped us load all our luggage into their van. I was in a state of exhilaration as we drove through the bustling city. For twenty years I had longed to travel and especially to see Australia, where both my parents were born. Finally, I had made it! It was exciting, realising that Josh and I could explore the city to our heart's delight for ten days.

After a quick catch up with Ian, we unpacked and I sorted through a pouch of documents. My first priority in Sydney was to visit the South African Embassy and find out why our study visas for South Africa had been denied. These were crucial documents; without them we would not be able to enter South Africa or begin my missions training.

My family in New Zealand had been very concerned when our

passports were returned to us without the visas, just two days before our departure. I knew with certainty that God was calling me to mission's work in Africa and trusted Him to sort this problem out before we left Sydney in ten days. After ringing the Embassy, I discovered that it would close in a few days for the three weeks annual Christmas break. We needed a miracle, and fast.

Joshua and I located the South African Embassy, a solid building with few windows and a small buzzer next to the wooden door. When I pressed the buzzer a stern male voice asked me what I wanted. I explained, and he unlocked the door. It all felt like something out of a cloak and dagger movie!

At the top of the stairs, a man was waiting for us behind a solid partition with a glass window. It was such a formal, serious atmosphere that I began to feel intimidated. I quickly explained our situation and after a short wait, Josh was instructed to wait while I was ushered into an office to meet someone named Henk, who turned out to be a friendly man. He listened carefully while I explained about sending all the requested documents, waiting for weeks, and then being informed that the study visas had all been declined. Henk's expression was caring and sympathetic, which gave me hope that he would help us. After looking up my application on his files, Henk told me that one of the required documents was missing. He explained that Home Affairs in Pretoria, South Africa was an enormous building, with many offices and departments, so sometimes documents became separated from application forms. He reassured me that he would ring the embassy that evening as they were eight hours behind Australian time. Henk then began chatting about his country, which helped me to relax and trust that he was committed to helping us. I thanked him for his help and set off with Josh to explore Sydney.

Joshua was familiar with the layout of the city centre as he had holidayed with his father when he was younger and had bussed around the city each day while his dad was at work. He knew where the popular tourist sites were and led me straight to the monorail. It only cost two dollars for a round trip, which went high above the city and stopped regularly at different tourist attractions. The sleek, modern, monorail was fast, quiet, and gave clear views of the city centre, the harbour, and the famous Paddy's Market. My father used to buy us all gifts at Paddy's Market whenever he sailed to Sydney, so it was a significant place for me. One year he bought me a terrapin tortoise that he smuggled home in his jacket pocket. Josh and I stopped at Centre Point Tower, then whizzed to the top in a lift and gazed out as the tower slowly revolved. The view was incredible, with the whole harbour and iconic buildings clearly visible all around.

Downstairs, an artist cut out our silhouettes very quickly on black paper. At a gift shop, we bought presents for the family and then got back on the monorail and headed for Darling Harbour. Joshua had a keen sense of direction and the confidence to match. He was enjoying being my tour guide!

Darling Harbour had a huge shopping complex which overloaded my senses. Hundreds of people were bustling about, shopping, eating, and chatting. I was fascinated by all the different nationalities around me and the laid back approach to life that was evident in people's casual clothes and mannerisms. The hot, muggy weather sapped my energy quickly, but the excitement of seeing the sights kept me going. Even though it was getting late we made a visit to the impressive Aquarium where we watched huge, sleek sharks and enormous, graceful stingrays floating above our heads as we walked through a glass tunnel beneath them. At 5:00 p.m., we reached home. Ian and Jenny were amazed at all we had accomplished in the heatwave!

The next morning, Henk rang to inform me that the missing document was the custody order for my sons. Thankfully I had made copies of all the application forms and was able to take the missing one to Henk immediately. He faxed it straight through to Pretoria.

There was a story to that particular document, as I had never been to court to obtain custody for my sons. There had been no need, as both of their fathers had moved overseas to different countries, leaving me to raise the boys alone. When I first applied for the study visa, there wasn't time to organize an official document because I didn't know

Mike's whereabouts, so I improvised with the help of a local Justice of the Peace. He typed up a document stating that I had full custody of both the boys and had been their sole caregiver for the past ten years. He signed it with a flourish and then applied several official-looking stamps to add weight to the document that I then sent with my visa application. As the embassy was closing the next day, I was well aware that we needed a miracle. I was comforted, knowing so many friends were praying for our plight; I felt deeply that our visas would be granted. The next stop in our journey would be London, but I decided we should visit the French Embassy to apply for visas, just in case the opportunity arose to jump across the channel to Europe. We had to quickly visit a local pharmacy to get passport-sized photos for the visas. It was an absolute relief to be inside air-conditioned buildings as we were wilting outside in the oppressive forty-degree heat. Back at the office, our passports were stamped with new visas for Europe. At least we had them, even if the idea of travelling to France seemed far-fetched and unrealistic at that stage.

Now all the official business was completed, we were ready to head for the famous Taronga Zoo that my mother had spoken about for many years. Her father had taken her there as a child. It was exciting for me to retrace her steps and visit places that were special to her. To get to the zoo, we needed to take a ferry. This was a treat for me.

We stood outside as the ferry made its way across the harbour, the wind blowing in our faces and the water spraying up the sides of the ferry. I felt so liberated and was bursting with happiness. After many stressful months of selling our home and disposing of most of our belongings, I was now able to relax and enjoy being a tourist. I no longer had the myriad of responsibilities that accompany being a single parent and running a home for two lads. I felt incredibly blessed and happy to be sharing these experiences with Joshua. Family holidays had been few and far between due to limited resources, although my older sister Margy had generously provided us with several trips to Auckland over the years. She was a caring and kind person, who realised that life was difficult for us at times and made sure we had some regular fun holidays with her family.

As we sailed across the harbour we had a great view of the famous Sydney Opera House, which was shaped like a shell, and the iconic Sydney Harbour Bridge. My mother was pushed in a pram across the bridge by her father on the opening day in the 1930s. As we disembarked, we made our way to a gondola that gave us an aerial view of the zoo. Wow, another unique ride!

We spent the day exploring the fascinating zoo. For five dollars we had our photos taken with a koala, an actual live, cuddly bear! By the end of the day, we had sore feet but more importantly, we had many photos and happy memories.

The next day was the last chance we had to get our visas before we flew to London. We were all praying for a breakthrough. When we arrived at the embassy, Henk greeted me with a smile. The permits had all been issued! Henk asked for some photos for our visas, and I was thankful that, coincidentally, we had some extra ones from our European visa applications. Henk considered sending Eli's papers to Zimbabwe but then changed his mind. Instead, he asked me for a photo of Eli. With a sinking heart, I realised I didn't have any and then wondered if this would jeopardize Eli's visa process.

Suddenly, I remembered that my friend Bev, who had helped me prepare for the trip, had told me to photocopy our passports before we left. I had Eli's copy in my bag. Henk produced some scissors and deftly cut out Eli's photo to attach to the file. He then handed over all three visas. I was so relieved and excited that I gave him a big hug. Henk had been an immense support and help to us during a tense and hurried process.

The timing of our visas being issued was incredible, as the embassy closed the next day for the Christmas holidays. I was very grateful to Henk for his diligence and kindness towards us and also grateful to God for sorting out the situation so wonderfully. We could now enjoy the rest of our time in Sydney with the assurance that we had the necessary documents to enter South Africa in January. That evening, Ian and Jenny joined us in prayer, thanking God for his faithfulness and perfectly timed help.

After a few days of sightseeing, we decided to track down Josh's father, Mike, who lived in Sydney with his partner, Annette, and their young daughter, Pearl. When Josh was nine he had spent time in Sydney with Mike and Annette during the school holidays. Each day, Mike took Josh to the worksite where he was erecting scaffolding and then encouraged him to bus into the city to see the sights. After an adventurous day, Joshua would catch the bus back to his father's workplace, sharing all his experiences as they travelled home. I felt it was important for Joshua to spend time with his Dad before we emigrated to the other side of the world.

Joshua remembered that Annette worked at a hospital close to their home, so we looked on a map, drew a wide circle around their suburb and located the hospitals within the circle. The names weren't familiar to Josh, so I jotted down several possibilities and looked up the phone numbers in a gigantic Sydney phone book.

During the day, while Josh and I were sightseeing, I began to ring the list of numbers. I knew it was a long shot as Annette could have changed her job in the past seven years, but we were trusting God to connect us. Much to my surprise and relief, I was put through to her at the second hospital I rang! They had been waiting for us to contact them, she said, as my younger brother, Peter, had told them we were coming to Sydney. I was excited that we had found them so easily.

Annette and Mike invited us to stay for a few days and celebrate Christmas with them. Joshua was keen, so I accepted the invitation, recognizing that this was an opportunity he might not have again for a long time. We spent an enjoyable time together visiting their friends, sightseeing and buying some presents for each other. Mike was awkward at first but surprised me by sincerely asking for forgiveness for his part in our painful marriage. I had forgiven him long ago, so I was able to reciprocate the feelings. I told him we were both so young when we married that we were clueless about how to handle the challenges we faced. With that conversation out of the way, Mike relaxed noticeably, and we were able to simply enjoy the experience of us all being together. Pearl was a love-able little girl who held my hand as we walked around and chatted away easily as young children do.

On our last evening, as Annette and I prepared a meal together, I asked her how she was coping with me being in her home and especially with Mike being so attentive to me. I wondered how she was handling this situation. Annette surprised me by saying that she was fine with it and felt that Mike needed this time with me to lay some things to rest from his past. A wise lady!

The next morning, I quietly reflected on the past few days with them and remembered how hesitant I had been initially, but it had been a very special time of healing and bonding. I had sensed God's presence throughout. He had turned a potentially awkward time into one of closeness and blessing.

Joshua was also unusually quiet. After years of not seeing his Dad, they had bonded strongly again and now Josh had to say goodbye with the knowledge that he wouldn't be seeing his Dad again for some years. This was very hard on him. It was an emotional time for us all as we said goodbye.

Meanwhile, Eli's trip to Zimbabwe proved to be a lot more challenging than I had imagined. He had never stayed away from Joshua and me before and he suddenly found himself in an entirely different culture where the food, language, and people were all new to him. Although my intention was for him to spend time getting to know his father and his African heritage, in hindsight I realised that we should have all travelled together and gone to Zimbabwe at a later stage. It was a stressful time for me knowing I had put Eli into this situation and was too far away to be able to help him cope with the culture shock and loneliness he was experiencing. After some homesick phone calls, I was relieved to hear him sounding happier. He told me about the photos he had been taking of the monkeys and chameleons in the trees at the back of the house. The antics of the monkey troops passing through the garden daily were highly amusing to him. I was grateful to Solomon and his family for doing their best to help Eli to adjust to a completely different world. Relieved that he was now happier, I began to focus on the next part of the journey.

All too soon it was time to begin the long flight to London. My brother Donald, who I hadn't seen for ten years, was meeting us at the airport with his wife, Stephanie. A special highlight of the flight was when the pilot announced that we were about to fly over Moscow. Since it was 4 a.m. most passengers were sleeping, but the cramped seats had kept me awake. I lifted the window shutter and peeked out into the black night sky. As I gazed downwards I was rewarded with an incredibly beautiful sight. It appeared as though someone had generously sprinkled bright, twinkling diamonds on a bed of black velvet. I was mesmerized as we flew over this enormous city, where the lights from factories, buildings, and highways created a spectacular sight to those of us flying high above this medieval city.

After enjoying the hot, sunny weather of Sydney, we were not prepared for the biting cold and gloominess of London. It was quite a drastic shock to go from summer to winter in one day. Thankfully we had brought a few warm clothes with us. After going through customs, we walked into the arrivals area, expecting to be greeted by Donald and Steph. I was confident they would be waiting for us, but they were nowhere to be seen. After the first half-hour of watching everyone who entered the area, I realised they must have been unexpectedly delayed. By now I was desperately tired and longing for a hot breakfast and a comfy bed to help me get over jet lag. After waiting for over two hours the tension grew between Joshua and me, and we began to lose patience with each other. Joshua was fully convinced I had not sent the correct details to Donald. Eventually, after two and a half hours, they arrived without any explanation for the enormous delay.

We boarded a train to the suburb where they lived. I was fascinated to watch as passengers on the cramped carriage stared straight ahead over the tops of other passenger's heads. Some people read a book but the majority sat quietly for the whole trip. There was virtually no conversation going on; people avoided eye contact or interaction with the person next to them. This was the complete opposite of Australian behaviour, where strangers often greeted me and struck up a conversation while we were travelling. I was amused by some bus drivers addressing elderly women as "love" while asking them about their day. As I sat on the train, I didn't realise I was witnessing the typical behaviour of people who live in a cold climate. They are typically more private and reserved, but to me it all felt uncomfortable and unfriendly. Everything looked dull and gloomy. The much-anticipated daylight only began in mid-morning, and then quickly disappeared by mid-afternoon. London was the exact opposite of the long, hot, sunny days of Sydney. We planned to stay with Donald and Steph for several days, but I soon realised that our time together wasn't going to be fruitful or positive, mainly due to wounds he still carried from the past. After two days I felt we needed to move on, but didn't know where to go. I prayed for guidance and was surprised by God's answer for us.

The next morning, as Joshua and I passed through a small shopping centre, I glanced up at a large colourful poster in the window of a travel agent. The picture was of the Eiffel Tower in Paris with an offer of return ferry tickets to France for ten pounds. Now that I had finally begun travelling and had seen how fascinating and different each country was, I decided Paris was our next stop; after all, we already had visas. I turned to Joshua and said, "Let's go to France," but he was not keen on the idea. I definitely was, so without hesitation or further discussion, I bought two return tickets and felt thrilled that we were about to visit mainland Europe. This was not part of the original plan, but it seemed like too good an opportunity to miss. What an enormous adventure this trip was turning into!

The local bank, unfortunately, didn't have any French francs available, but it did have some Belgium francs. I bought those, figuring they might come in handy at some point in our travels, but I was confident that we could buy some local currency in Paris.

That night I announced to Donald and Steph that we were off to Europe in the morning. He looked surprised and was perhaps relieved, but Steph quietly apologised to me for his behaviour. She had been kind and hospitable to us. Because we had limited funds, I packed a jar of gherkins and some mayonnaise, along with a sharp knife into a separate bag. I planned to buy bread and cheese wherever we went.

The next day we took a bus to the ferry terminal and then boarded the ferry bound for Calais. It was absolutely fascinating watching passengers from many different parts of the world. This was our first experience being amongst so many Indian, Pakistani, and Chinese people, some of whom were speaking fluent French. My mind was abuzz with all these new sights and sounds. The funniest sight was of a middle-aged African-American lady who opened up a bag and began putting large, brightly coloured, plastic curlers into her hair. This was obviously part of her nightly routine, which she accomplished very quickly. While I was unable to snooze at all, she lay down on a long hard bench and fell asleep effortlessly.

Once we reached Calais, we transferred onto a bus, which I assumed was taking us into Paris. As it was late at night, we dozed while the bus sped through the countryside. To my surprise, when the bus stopped at 6:00 a.m., I looked out of the window and realised we were not in the city at all, but on the outskirts of a small town.

As the passengers began to disembark, I realised we needed help; I didn't have any francs to purchase food or even to buy bus tickets to Paris. I decided to give a big smile as I scanned the passengers, waiting to see who responded. Thankfully, a young, friendly lady smiled back at me. After telling her our plight, she invited us to travel with her and her

Left: Sydney Harbour

Right: Mike and I with Josh and his little sister in our visit to Australia

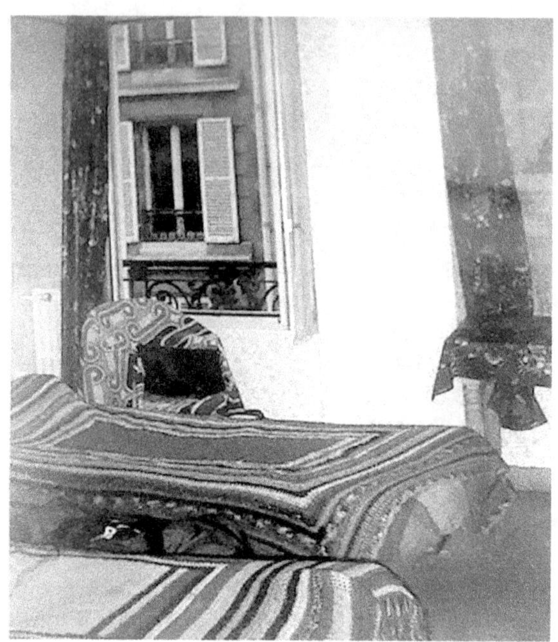

Our 'budget' accommodation with sagging beds

A cold winter's day in Holland

sister. They were Irish and visiting Paris for a quick trip so the younger sister could collect her belongings from her ex-boyfriend's flat. The resourceful older sister took us under her wing, bought multiple bus tickets for us, and paid for a cheap breakfast for Josh and me at a small sidewalk café. Her sister was diabetic and needed a substantial meal, so they set off to find a restaurant with the promise they would be back to join us.

What an incredible feeling to be in Paris! I had only ever seen it in the movies or on TV, and now here we were, enjoying croissants and strong coffee while watching the smartly dressed Parisians walk quickly by on their way to work. This was a normal weekday for them, but my life was changing and expanding by the hour. The small town single mother from obscure Coniston, New Zealand, had become an international traveller. I savoured every moment of this epic adventure.

An hour later the Irish sisters returned and took us to a cheap, rustic pension (rooms to let) where an elderly lady led us up several flights of curving stone stairs to our bedroom on the third floor. We tried not to laugh when we entered the room; it looked like something from the 1950s, with crocheted bed covers in colourful squares. Once the proprietor had gone, Josh and I decided to try out the two metal single beds to assess how comfortable they were. We roared with laughter when the middles sagged so badly that our bums almost hit the floor! All I could see of Josh was his head on the pillow, his feet sticking up at the other end, and most of his body curved into a 'U' in the middle. To access the shower, I had to go back down the spiraling stairs to pay the proprietor a small sum of money, and then race back up two flights, and locate the small shower room. There was not a second to waste as the hot water I had paid for was restricted to only a few minutes! Once inside I washed quickly and vigorously before the hot water suddenly ended and cold water blasted onto my unsuspecting body.

The Irish sisters had lent me enough money to pay for two nights, with the promise that I would pay them back as soon as the banks opened up. The sisters acted as guides, taking us to the famous Notre Dame cathedral, which had magnificent paintings throughout. I marvelled that the cathedral had survived all the bombings and destruction of World War II. At the end of the second day, we said goodbye to our Irish guardian angels who had taken such good care of the two novice tourists from "down under."

By now, I was realising it was quite simple to travel around Europe with the extensive rail network, and also that several countries were close to Paris. Thinking that this trip might possibly be the only time we would visit Europe, I suggested to Josh that we take a train to Belgium and then Holland as both countries had Youth With A Mission (YWAM) training bases with accommodation for travellers. Finally enjoying our grand adventure, Josh agreed, so after a brief phone call, we were booked into the Brussels base for one night and then the Amsterdam base for four nights.

Youth With A Mission is the largest missions training organization in the world, with training bases in over one hundred countries. I had been accepted to train with them in South Africa for six months before I was to venture out into townships to begin community development work amongst the poor. I was so thankful that we had not flown straight to Cape Town from New Zealand. This trip was developing into something far more than I had anticipated.

My eyes were glued to the window as we sped north through France and on into Belgium. I rang the YWAM base once we got off at the train station to tell them we had arrived, but to my surprise, I found we had exited at the wrong station! We boarded the next train and arrived at the correct station within minutes.

The building where the YWAM missionaries lived and worked was magnificent, with mirror-lined walls and a stunning wide-curved wooden staircase. The staff told us the premises had been an upmarket bridal salon for many years, hence all the grandeur and floor to ceiling mirrors down the curved staircase. After an afternoon of sightseeing and a good night's sleep, we set off for the next leg of the journey, which would take us by train to Amsterdam.

As a child, I had a Dutch friend at primary school, so being able to visit her country was particularly significant to me. I loved all the different lace curtains in the windows of the tall buildings we passed, and of course the magnificent, iconic windmills dotted across the landscape. Because it was January and the middle of winter, there was not one tulip to be seen, but I could imagine how glorious the landscape would appear once they were all in bloom. The myriad of canals amazed me, as did the hundreds of people riding bicycles. Once we were settled into our guest room at the De Poort YWAM base, we were invited downstairs for a wonderful complimentary hot meal. What a relief to have something different from bread, gherkins and cheese!

The next day we were up bright and early, eager to explore this historic city. It was an incredible feeling walking on streets that were hundreds of years old and full of history. I drank in all the sights, tasted as much of the local food as possible, and chatted to anyone who looked friendly. At the YWAM base, Josh met a young lad his age whose parents were originally from America but had been missionaries in Amsterdam for many years. They worked with people trapped in lifestyles of addiction to drugs and dangerous behaviours. Josh spent two days with his new friend and returned excitedly to the base on the second evening declaring that he had been invited to become the drummer for an outreach team going to Russia. I, of course, was taken completely by surprise; my teenage son who had been reluctant to leave New Zealand was now expecting me to wave him goodbye as he set off for Russia! He was not at all happy with me when I ended his dream by reminding him we were actually heading for Africa, not Russia. I was fascinated to see how easily he was making friends in foreign cultures and how confident he was at 16, prepared to head off without any family for a new experience in a very cold and challenging country.

The next day Josh and I reluctantly began our return journey to England. We were both lost in thought, processing everything we had seen and experienced during our impromptu detour into Europe. Once there, the last two days in London whizzed by. We met up with friends from Coniston who took us to see the London Bridge and Madam Tussaud's Wax Museum. In the city centre, the bay windows of large department stores displayed marvellous Christmas-themed scenes. At each window, throngs of people gathered on the pavements, admiring the skilled presentations.

Soon it was time for our final flight, which would take us from London to Cape Town, South Africa, and to the start of our new life. The boys would attend local schools while I began my training as a missionary with YWAM.

As we flew from London to Cape Town I felt overwhelmed at God's goodness to me. For ten years, I had been aware of His specific call on my life to work as a missionary amongst vulnerable people in Africa, but I had no idea how this would come about.

During these years I had sometimes been ridiculed for wanting to go to Africa, which caused me to occasionally resent this calling. Few people understood my determination to leave New Zealand and take the boys to an unknown continent. A pastor at one church I attended even remarked while preaching about "these people who aren't coping and want to run away to Africa." I regularly felt humiliated and lonely, but fortunately I had wonderful friends who encouraged me when I was discouraged.

I had suffered most of my life with insecurity and low self-esteem, and knew that, in reality, I was the most unlikely person God could have chosen to train as a missionary and serve Him in Africa. Having read many missions books, I was aware that He often chose seemingly insignificant and unlikely people to do extraordinary things as He guided and provided for them every step of the way. I wasn't at all sure how our time in Africa would unfold, or even what I would do once my training was finished, but I was confident that God had it all planned out. I just needed to keep moving ahead and listen to Him as He guided me into my destiny.

I had embarked on this unknown journey with determination. The confident woman I was becoming was so different from the insecure and anxious little girl and young woman I had always been. God was not merely preparing me to love and serve others. His love was also healing me from my own deep scars.

CHAPTER TWO

Where Do I Belong?

1953 - 1959

Like any child, I longed to feel safe and loved by caring parents, but instead I lacked a meaningful sense of connection to my own family. My maternal grandmother had died when Mum was four and Mum's father died when she was twelve. Mum had an excellent education and was adored by her father's sister and the mother superior of the Catholic secondary school she attended. A gifted pianist, Mum trained and passed all her exams to the level of a concert pianist.

After a sheltered upbringing, Mum met Dad, who was a sailor just like her beloved father. They married and moved to his parent's home in Port Lyttleton, near Christchurch, just as a huge national strike was beginning. For a year there was little money available. This made life difficult, and even more so when their first baby arrived.

My father's upbringing was the complete opposite of Mum's. His father had been away during the six years of World War II. Meanwhile, Dad and his three teenage brothers were skipping school and making up their own rules for life. After a few years of marriage, my father became verbally abusive and aggressive. This was a new experience for my mother, who had been adored by her parents and her aunt all her life. She coped by doing things the way Dad wanted and staying silent when he was angry—anything to keep from making waves. Taking long walks with her German shepherd, Karl, gave Mum some precious time away from the tension and criticism at home.

In my early years, I was angry with my mother for not protecting me from Dad's anger, not realising she was probably overwhelmed as well. Mum had been diagnosed with cancer in her early twenties, which resulted in major surgery. Thankfully Mum survived, but without parents or siblings to discuss her problems with, I imagine she experienced long periods of loneliness. In that era, people rarely shared personal situations with anyone outside their family.

Over time, as I watched my father interacting with my brothers and sisters it became clear that he felt differently towards me. I had no idea why he targeted me when venting his frustration and anger. My siblings seemed to enjoy a relatively easier childhood. As I grew older, I often referred to myself as the black sheep of the family. But I did have an escape. My paternal Nana was my one safe place during these turbulent childhood years. I often stayed with her on weekends or holidays. The feelings of safety, belonging and being loved were powerful. My grandfather was away at sea for months at a time, so Nana and I had the double bed to ourselves. We spent many a dark winter's night reading books and drinking copious cups of tea. One of her friends made pickled onions which I adored and devoured by the jar.

During stormy nights when thunder was roaring in the turbulent skies, the loud crack of lightening caused Nana to panic and push me under the blankets, where I was told to search for and remove the metal hair clips from my hair. Nana believed that lightning could strike me in bed because of the offending hair clips. I believed her, of course, and was always relieved to not be struck down during a storm. Once the potentially dangerous hair clips were removed, I was free again to sit up, drink tea and munch on delicious, crunchy pickled onions.

When I was five, I decided that I needed to take some action and find another home, so I began to ask relatives to adopt me. The first person I approached was my father's youngest brother, Uncle Martin. He was a swashbuckling figure, riding his deer culling horse from the mountain region of Hanmer Springs to our city. After navigating the busy city streets, he would tie his horse up to the lamppost in front of our home and come in to visit. I quite fancied saying farewell to my family and riding off into the sunset with Uncle Martin because he seemed to have such an adventurous life. He wasn't married and had no children of his own, so I anticipated being the centre of his attention. In my five-year-old opinion, Uncle Martin would make the perfect father for me. And so, during one of his visits I waited for him to finish talking with Mum and Dad in the lounge and then I signalled to him to come into the hallway where I quickly whispered my idea to him. Alas, he didn't take to the idea as eagerly as I had hoped he would.

My next hope was my beloved Nana. I knew with certainty that she loved me deeply. Nana understood my desire to get away from home but was intimidated by my father, so she declined the invitation and I stopped looking for a new home. It had not been as easy as I thought it would be, so I moved on from that idea.

When I was seven years old my parents built a lovely four-bedroom house on a quarter-acre property. The area we lived in was developing, so at the time there were many new homes. Neighbours got to know one another quickly, especially since there were no fences dividing the different properties. The Collins, an English couple with two young sons, owned the property behind us. When an adjoining fence was built between our place and theirs, my father put a gate in so we could visit each other easily. Little did we know that this small act would change my life forever.

My mum became good friends with Mrs. Collins, visiting her often in their home. While Mum was visiting the Collinses in the evenings, she

Me, at age 6

My Nana

*Left: My
natural
parents*

*Right: Us five
kids (with me
on the left)*

would quickly pop over to check on us. After some time, Mr. Collins offered to do this for her. Even then, Mrs. Collins never revealed the fact that her husband was a pedophile. He was free to charm and befriend the grownups while beginning to 'groom' their children. Consequently, for a whole year, whenever Dad was away at sea, Mr. Collins molested me. Sometimes he would even molest me when I was at his home playing with his sons. His wife was also present in their home, but she chose not to intervene. As a small child, I didn't understand what he was doing to me, all I knew was that something scary was happening.

My older sister, Margy, told me in later years that I always protected her and made sure Mr. Collins never came near her. As I slept on the bottom bunk, Mr. Collins had easier access to me, and apparently, when he began to move towards Margy in the top bunk I would say something to distract him. In this way, she was spared the confusing and damaging experiences I went through. Eventually, as Mum was leaving one night to visit Mrs. Collins, Margy forcefully told Mum not to go and then tearfully told her what had been happening. To my Mum's credit, she marched straight over to the couple and confronted them.

My brave Mum laid charges immediately. I remember being taken to the police station for an in-depth interview with a kind policeman. The local families were apparently unaware that Mr. Collins was a disgraced British Army Officer who had been discharged for molesting small children in India. Mrs. Collins later told my Mum that she had planned to move to New Zealand, buy a house, and then divorce Mr. Collins. She was a calculating woman who conveniently ignored the danger to all the local children. Instead, she prioritized and focused on her financial security. Mrs. Collins's silence and subsequent cover-up of her husband's behaviour facilitated the trauma I experienced. Her indirect role in what happened damaged me deeply as a young child. My mother told me that I had always been an outgoing, friendly and very trusting child until I was molested. After that, I was wary of men and quite reticent.

After the court case, Mr. Collins went to prison for a year while life carried on much the same at home. When Mr. Collins was released from prison, the police were concerned for my safety and advised my father to quit his job at sea and work on the land. Dad had been a sailor since his mid-teens and hated working on land; this was not an easy decision for him. He coped by spending weekends out with his mates, drinking and playing darts. Unfortunately for us, he would often arrive home in a drunken bad mood and begin berating Mum or us kids.

One of our neighbours who was a policeman found out that I had been molested and he mentioned it to Dad. Knowing that our family secret was now public knowledge made Dad livid with me. He began accusing me of "bringing shame on our family." As an eight-year-old, I believed him. I felt defective and alone because I had brought great shame to our family. I was confused and couldn't work out why I deserved so much hostility from my father, so I concluded that it was all my fault.

The fear of Mr. Collins coming to punish me when he got out of prison, coupled with Dad's growing anger and verbal abuse, caused me to become anxious and fearful, especially at night. Lying in bed, looking into the dark shadowy room, I regularly imagined that I saw a man crawling along the floor with a knife, coming towards me. The fear caused panic attacks which impaired my breathing. One night, when it all became too much for me and I was gasping for breath, I must have called out. My Dad appeared in my room and he asked me what was happening. I told him about the man with the knife and in a rare show of kindness he told me that I didn't need to fear, as he was in the house and would protect me.

For decades I regularly dreamed that men were chasing me through streets in a strange place. I was desperately trying to fly above them, clutching at my clothing so that they couldn't grab it and pull me down. Another frequent nightmare also began with me running from a group of dangerous men. In a state of terror, I would frantically search for an open door in houses or shops, yelling out for help, but no one responded. They all watched and ignored my plight. Sometimes shopkeepers would pretend to hide me, then simply hand me over to my tormentors. These were the two main dreams that filled my nights with terror and anxiety for many decades.

As our home life became more unpleasant and unpredictable, my four siblings and I found other families to spend time and occasionally stay with. These families provided us with an escape from the tensions at home. During my ninth year, when I was staying with Nana, I met a lady called Margaret at the corner shop. Nana had sent me to buy some butter, and being a friendly child I began talking to other customers. Margaret offered to give me a lift across town from my Nana's house back to my home on Sunday and I agreed. On Sunday evening Nana waved goodbye as this kind stranger drove off with me. Little did I know, I was about to experience a dramatic spiritual awakening.

Instead of driving me straight home, Margaret said we were going to stop in the city and listen to a man called Peter Morrow. He was an Australian pastor whom God had directed to Christchurch to begin a new movement. Peter led people into the baptism of the Holy Spirit, with accompanying signs and wonders following. At the meeting I saw about twenty people sitting in a circle, watching as a skinny man instructed a young man to sit on a chair. Peter explained that this man had ongoing back pain. To our surprise, we watched as Peter held both his feet in the palms of his hands and showed us that one leg was shorter than the other. As we all watched, Peter commanded the short leg to grow in Jesus's name, and to our amazement, the leg grew! Both legs were now the same length. Another person with back pains asked for prayer and we watched as they were also healed.

By the time Margaret dropped me off at my home, the house was in darkness apart from the front porch light. I excitedly burst into my parent's bedroom and described everything I had seen. Dad wasn't impressed, but Mum sat up and listened to it all. Unbeknownst to me, she later attended these early sessions of the newly formed New Life Church that spread throughout New Zealand, and had a huge spiritual awakening of her own.

That one experience of seeing God heal people transformed the way I had always viewed Him. In my child's mind, He was a stern policeman with a big stick who was watching me to see when I did something wrong. God seemed to be a punitive, demanding figure. After hearing Peter teach about God and explaining how He longs for relationship and to heal His people, I saw God as a kind, miracle-working, loving Father.

CHAPTER THREE

I Am Special to Someone

1965 - 1970

During the 1960s my world was filled with fabulous music from The Beatles, The Beach Boys, Stevie Wonder, Diana Ross and the Supremes, Gene Pitney, and Elvis Presley. Music brought me great joy. I also loved jokes and could find humour in most situations. I was much like any other girl at that time, but deep within me I had a growing sense that I was special to someone. I just didn't know who that someone was! At times I thought I had found them, but disappointingly this feeling was short-lived. My heart held hope and excitement about the journey ahead of me in spite of the unpleasantness around me.

At home, my father continued to vent his anger on me in unexpected and confusing ways. On Christmas day in 1966, just before my fourteenth birthday, my mother called all five of us children to the lounge to receive our much-anticipated gifts. I was excited as she showed me a lovely second-hand sewing machine she had bought for me. My mother gave great thought to our presents and most years paid them off over many months. As I had begun sewing my own clothes, the machine was a wonderful gift. For some reason, my father took offence. With intense rage, he snatched the sewing machine up and headed outside, threatening to smash it on the concrete patio. We followed him in disbelief, pleading with him to stop. Just as we all reached the back door, my older sister Margy appeared with a large knife and in a rare show of courage and outrage she told him that she was sick of the way he treated me. We were shocked at the scene unfolding before our eyes as Margy then told dad that she intended to run him through with the knife if he damaged my machine. As it was a long bread knife with a rounded end, there was not much chance of injury, but her desperate point was made. The violent actions and accusing words of his favourite child shocked Dad so much that he stopped in his tracks. He did however turn and proceeded to kick me in the back and send me to my room. Thankfully, my precious sewing machine was not destroyed.

Christmas morning passed with my family in the lounge opening presents and then having breakfast together, while I lay on my bed wondering why Dad hated me so much. The obvious reason for my young mind was that I must have been adopted and was therefore not his child at all. But I looked just like my younger sister and my mum, so I had to accept that adoption was not the reason for his rejection.

Soon thereafter, I decided to find work. I was tired of all the gathered skirts and the occasional dress I made with my limited abilities as a seamstress. With my sights on more fashionable clothes, I realised that I needed to earn money to turn my desires into a reality. Among the corner shops, near our home, an enterprising Dutchman, Kaase, had established a modern "milk bar" with booth seating like an American diner for those ordering hamburgers and milkshakes. Up until then, the only fast food available was fish and chips. Hamburgers were a novelty and very popular with the local teenagers. Kaase hired me for weekend work at the grand wage of four dollars a day. He cooked the hamburgers while I served customers and made the milkshakes, but he kept a close eye to make sure I didn't slip extra ice cream or flavouring into my friend's drinks. I felt quite grown up, earning my own money, as I no longer needed to rely on my parents for clothes. This meant I could choose any style of clothing that appealed to me.

During this time, a few boys from high school began asking me out on dates. I was nervous about being alone with any of them but eventually accepted an invitation to a movie with an older student called Malcolm. I felt intimidated by how handsome and self-assured he was, almost to the point of arrogance. He had a fabulous motorbike which I fancied a ride on, so against my better judgement, I went out with him. That evening I discovered that Malcolm was someone who took what he wanted with no regard for my feelings or protests. He found my reluctance to spend time with him in the following weeks quite amusing, without any understanding of the shock and trauma he had put me through. I became aware of just how vulnerable I was with teenage boys and young men, but lacked the knowledge or skills to protect myself. My self-esteem was very low throughout my teen years, a product of the belittling and abuse I had been through. The result of several negative experiences was a deep mistrust and almost hatred towards Pakeha (white) men. My conclusion at fourteen was that they were devious, selfish people and not to be trusted. It was only when I received counselling in my fifties that I learned that the molestation I had experienced had destroyed the boundaries that I was still forming as a child and a teen.

One of the families that I ran to when life became too hard at home was the Morris family. There are not many homes where the adults would let a teenage girl arrive unannounced and stay for a few days, without any contact from her parents. I found that the most obliging people were those who were also struggling, perhaps with an alcoholic partner or as a single parent trying to provide for their children. For some reason, they were more flexible and accommodating to someone else in need. One dark, rainy night when I was afraid I was about to be hit by dad, I ran barefoot down our street until I reached the Morris home to see Naomi, a school friend. Her mother had escaped from a violent marriage and brought her four children to our city the previous year. Mrs. Morris was a strong Maori lady who ran her home like clockwork. I was always made to feel welcome. On Saturday nights, she spent most of her time with her new partner and friends socialising, so Naomi and I would stay at the house to babysit the younger children.

Over time, I started to notice that Naomi lied to her mother about secret outings she made at night. For example, Naomi would ask me to go to the movies with her on a Friday night, but when we got to the theatre, she would give me two tickets and tell me to watch the movie alone and wait for her to return. Once home, Naomi would show her mother the movie tickets, covering her tracks each time. I was disturbed by her behaviour, but at a loss on how to handle this situation. I didn't want to deceive Mrs. Morris, but I also didn't want to lose my main friend whose family had become my second home, so I spent a year accompanying her to parties or the movies and then often spending the evenings alone.

During my sixteenth year, I was studying for the University Entrance exams at high school. My English teacher and softball coach was Miss Robertson. She was a warm person with whom I felt safe sharing my struggles at home. I can't remember exactly how it came about, but one day after school, Miss Robertson took me home to her flat and told me I was staying with her. This was exciting for me! I imagined myself arriving at school each morning on the back of Miss Robertson's scooter. To my surprise, the next morning she took me to a Maori girls' hostel called Roseneath, which was across town from where I lived. Roseneath was a large, two-storey home that had been converted into a hostel for rural girls who moved into the city to do an apprenticeship. The matron showed me to the room that I would be sharing with two older girls. Miss Robertson took me home to collect some clothes, and that was the last time I saw her. My education had come to an abrupt end. At the time this didn't seem very significant to me because of the relief I felt at being out of my stressful home life and the thrill of starting a new adventure.

The next morning the matron told me I would need to find a job as I was required to pay board. This seemed reasonable to me, so I walked into the city and asked at the main post office if they had a vacancy. They didn't, but directed me upstairs to the international toll exchange where I was given a position immediately. I felt very grown-up working with a room full of adults and speaking with people all over the world! Even though the reality of my situation was that I had lost everything familiar to me, like school and living with my family, I was not overwhelmed or sad. My siblings told me that Dad was not happy that I had left home. I knew I wouldn't be visiting as he was unpredictable when he was angry. I discovered that I enjoyed being in new situations, especially when it included meeting strangers. I found people fascinating and made friends easily.

After a short stay at Roseneath, I left and rented a small flat with another girl. Our only furnishings consisted of two mattresses, some plates, cutlery, mugs, and one pot for cooking.

Since it was near Christmas and I couldn't go home, Mum agreed to come into the city by bus on Christmas Eve. This must have been very difficult for her emotionally. When she arrived, Mum gave me a hug, and then we spent time catching up before exchanging gifts. All too soon, Mum was back on the bus heading for home to prepare for Christmas celebrations. It hit me afresh that I truly was not welcome in my own family because of Dad's attitude towards me. I walked back to my empty, bare flat in the early evening with a deep sense of aloneness, not looking forward to spending Christmas Eve on my own. To my surprise, late in the evening, a friend's older brother knocked at my door and asked if I wanted to spend the evening on the bread run with him. I was delighted to have company after all, so I enthusiastically agreed and jumped into his warm van. We headed off to the main bakery in another suburb to load up the orders of loaves, bread, and buns for his customers. For a few hours, he delivered people's Christmas orders into their letterbox cavities. Many people left gifts of chocolate, which he gave me, or beer, which he drank. Along the way, we found a stray kitten that I tucked under my jacket and cuddled on the journey. My kind bread delivery friend dropped me back home in the early hours of the morning. I curled up on my mattress with kitty purring beside me, feeling happy and content about my unexpected adventure. Christmas Day was spent alone with my new kitten.

A few months later, a girl I had spent time with on a fruit-picking holiday a year before asked me if I wanted to travel with her. I was bored with my job at the toll exchange and readily agreed. Jane was confident, resourceful, and had plenty of initiative. I was happy to go along with whatever plans she made for us. Jane had arranged for us to stay at a relative's flat in Wellington City, so a few days later we set off by train and ferry for the North Island, and then walked to the hospital where Jane had secured jobs for us in the laundry.

It only took one miserable day hauling heavy, wet washing from one tub to another before we both decided to quit this back-breaking, boring job. As work was plentiful, we applied for waitressing jobs at a tourist hotel in a national park and found this much more to our liking, even though it was a long way from the nearest town. The cook was an old man called Stan who managed to insert his name into the menu each week (Chicken a la Stan, Stan's Apple Crumble, etc.). The barman was a friendly person who offered to pierce my ears when I decided I quite fancied wearing earrings. Unfortunately, the only needle we could find was a large darning needle. He "cleansed" it by passing it through a flame and then instructed me to lean my head against the wooden door so I wouldn't move while he pushed the needle through my earlobe. I obeyed and after hearing a crunch and a bit of pain, I was the proud owner of pierced ears!

After waitressing for several months, my friend Naomi wrote to me inviting me to join her in a town called Waitotara, where she assured me I could easily find work and we could flat together. After the isolation of the national park, I thought the new place sounded great. I said farewell to Jane and took a long bus ride across the North Island, arriving late at night to begin my new life in the town of Waitotara. Naomi was waiting for me and showed me to our temporary home, which was across the road from the local pub. We were to stay with her cousin, Josy, and Josy's husband, Ron. With my savings from waitressing and a suitcase of lovely clothes I had recently bought, I felt confident that I would find an interesting job soon and that we could set up a small flat with the savings I earned.

That all changed the next morning when I woke up and looked outside. I was expecting to see a bustling town. Instead, I was shocked to see I was in a small country village beside a river with only a pub, a grocery store, a butchery and a post office. This town was smaller than the proverbial one-horse town! With a sinking feeling in the pit of my gut, I realised that Naomi had lured me here under false pretenses. There were no flats in sight and the only available work consisted of back-breaking potato-picking. After my initial disappointment, I decided to make the best of the situation and began the dirty work of plucking potatoes from freshly turned soil. Thankfully a few weeks later, a sewing factory opened up in the next town and I began working there.

On the weekends, the young men from Waitotara and nearby towns arrived at the local pub to begin a weekend of partying. Once they had their pay, they headed straight for the pub to sing, drink, play pool, and enjoy themselves. The local girls joined them, myself included, then cooked for them when the party moved at closing time to Ron and Jane's compact house. I made new friends and enjoyed the relaxed, friendly, happy atmosphere that was typical of each weekend. On Sundays everyone lounged around, slept, or returned to their homes. On Mondays, they returned to work to earn more money for the following weekend's celebrations. Oh, the joys of being young and single.

During that year I spent a few months on my favourite Uncle Martin's farm. His wife Joyce needed a break from milking morning and evening and they asked me to help out. I loved being with them as they were a hard-working but relaxed couple who enjoyed having fun. Uncle Martin was business-minded, so he told me he had organized a part-time job for me after I finished the morning milking. He introduced me to Jules, the family's horse, whose job it was to take me to a neighbouring farm to help a young single farmer called Brian for about two hours a day. Jules had no intention of assisting, but instead headed for the barbed wire fence along the roadside and rubbed my leg up close to it. I, of course, jumped off him to avoid being injured by the wire and each morning the farmer would be waiting with a grin on his face, saying "I knew you would be along soon as Jules is already here!" I found this humiliating and was determined each morning to show Jules I was the boss. Eventually, I gave up and walked instead. Turns out, Jules was the boss!

Brian had flaming red hair and a face full of freckles. He was friendly but awkward around me. My first job was taking a handful of crystals from a bucket and dropping them on to large weeds in his fields. This was the most tedious job I had ever done. By the second week, Brian was looking more at ease. When I asked him what he wanted me to do that day he startled me by replying, "I won't fight you if you want to join me in my bed!" Needless to say, I didn't go back there to work. Money didn't have that much appeal.

Another unpleasant event took place when my uncle hired me out to my aunty's brother Ken, who had a large sheep farm. Uncle Martin drove me over and introduced me to Ken and his family. They welcomed me and the wife, Anne, showed me to a comfortable room where I was to stay. For several days, Ken showed me how to milk the house cow by hand and how to feed the sheep. Then as they began lambing, I learned how to assist the ewes when their lambs got stuck during the birth process. It was mucky physical work, but I enjoyed learning new skills.

All was going well until one Friday evening when I came inside after milking the house cow and noticed that Anne and the children weren't there. Keith said he had sent them away for the weekend so we could be alone. It was only then that I realised he was wearing his pyjamas! I immediately rang my uncle on the house phone to tell him what was happening. Uncle Martin told me to pack my belongings and said he would come straight over to fetch me. He then asked to speak to Ken, who was looking quite subdued. I don't know what my Uncle said to his brother-in-law, but as we drove away Uncle Martin told me he had insisted that Ken paid me a full month's wages, plus an extra payment, even though I had only worked for about three weeks.

As a small child I had longed for Uncle Martin to rescue me from my home life and take me away with him on his horse. Instead, he was rescuing me at age seventeen in his old farm vehicle and saving me from another horrible experience. I was finding out that being a slim, pretty teenager had its drawbacks at times.

A month later I returned to Waitotara by bus. When I arrived in Wanganui, it was in the evening and I discovered there was no connecting bus until the next morning, so being resourceful I decided to hitchhike home. Even though it was dark, a driver spotted me and stopped. A friendly guy jumped out and offered me a seat in front next to the driver. He sat on the other side of me so I was between the two men. I started to feel a bit uncomfortable, but soon relaxed as they were friendly and chatted easily with me. However, as we approached Waitotara, the driver looked at me and said, "I think we will keep going, I like you." I realised I had a big problem on my hands.

Thinking quickly, in my most persuasive voice I said I thought that was a great idea but first could we just turn off the highway and stop at the Waitotara pub as I would like to introduce him to my friends. He was either not very smart or had a big ego, but either way, he agreed. As soon as we had disembarked, I made straight for the area where my friends would be drinking and playing pool. I headed for Sam Tamou, a tall, powerfully-built gentle giant and explained what had happened. Sam and a few others gave the two kidnappers some threatening looks and forced them to give me my suitcase from the boot of their car.

Without any violence, my would-be kidnappers could easily see they were outnumbered and quickly exited the pub, almost running to their car. I watched as their car sped away back up to the highway. I thanked my friends and walked across the road to where I was staying, realising I had just had a narrow escape. Hitch-hiking lost its appeal after that night!

As I settled back into Josy and Ron's home, I realised that things were not going very well. It was obvious that Josy was unhappy with her husband. In fact, after several uncomfortable weeks, I returned home from work one day to learn that Josy and Naomi had left and were now staying in another town with Josy's boyfriend! Ron had accepted the fact that they would not be returning. I was now alone with a lonely, upset, and abandoned man. The next night, he invited me to join him in his bed, but I naturally declined. Having no teeth and a pimply complexion did not make him an attractive person on a good day, plus he was a married man.

Once again I was in a predicament that I hadn't seen coming. I was angry at Naomi for lying to me and then abandoning me, and also angry at myself for believing her promises. I was not aware in those early years that the best predictor of a person's future behaviour is their past behaviour. I was now stuck in Ron's home, in a town where I knew few people, and I couldn't return home to Christchurch. Naturally, my thoughts turned toward my mother, but I knew I couldn't talk with her. During a recent bout of tonsillitis when I had been feeling low and wanted to talk with my mother, I had rung home. My oldest brother answered the call and then shocked me by saying that Dad had instructed them not to let me talk to Mum if I called. An overwhelming sense of rejection and aloneness swept over me. I was feeling physically vulnerable and in need of comfort. However, God was watching over me without my realising it, and He soon sent someone to rescue me.

A week after Naomi and Josy left, I heard a loud knock at the front door and when I opened it I saw Terry McGregor, the father of some of my new friends. He was an imposing man of gentle authority and said to me, "It is not good in this small town for a single girl to be living with a married man, so I am taking you to live with my family." This wonderful, wise Maori man had come with his two sons so they could carry my belongings to their house. As I had recently purchased a new divan bed with drawers underneath, I asked if we could take it with us. Much to the amusement of everyone looking on, an interesting procession took place as Terry led the way from Ron's home, up the main street and then down a side road to his own home. Terry carried my suitcase while his sons followed behind with my prized divan bed, and I brought up the rear carrying a smaller bag. Terry's wife April looked quite surprised as we entered their home, but quickly showed me to the two older girls' room and organized for one of the single beds to be replaced by my divan.

I shared a room with two of the daughters, Avian and Sylvia, and became an instant member of a large Maori family. I experienced a sense of safety and belonging that had been missing my whole life. Very quickly, I adapted to this new culture and embraced the customs that were explained to me. This experience laid the foundation for my ability to be flexible and adapt to different cultures in the years ahead. Terry McGregor became the father I never had. This brought much healing to my heart. My Maori mother was an incredible woman who willingly allowed me to join her large family and, over time, we became close. My heart soared one day when she introduced me to some friends as her "adopted daughter." By moving to the McGregor's home, I instantly gained thirteen siblings, all remarkable people whom I love deeply.

Chapter Four

Return to Christchurch

1971 – 1976

In my nineteenth year my paternal grandfather died in Christchurch. Consequently. I returned to my home city to be with my precious Nana. To my surprise, my father had softened so much towards me that I was allowed to live at home again. On occasions he was even affectionate towards me which made me feel we were finally connecting. Each day after my work at a chocolate factory, Dad would pick me up in his car. After handing him some fresh chocolates that should have been placed in a mixed assortments chocolate box but instead found their way into my pocket, we would chat about our day. I enjoyed our new relationship and felt accepted by him at last.

This softness ended quite abruptly one day when he found out that I was dating a Maori chap called Mike, a gentle humourous man. He had come down from the North Island and was training to be a panel beater as part of a government scheme to train young rural Maori in different trades. My father, like many people of that era, was prejudiced and wary of most other cultures. He became angry with me because of my relationship with Mike and soon after I found myself homeless again. I found a two-bedroom flat to rent and invited Mike and one of his friends to flat with me. We set up house together and after a few months I decided that the best way to gain a permanent sense of stability was to marry Mike. He agreed with my suggestion and three months later we were married. Dad had gradually got to know Mike and was no longer upset about our relationship. He agreed to drive me to the church and give me away. I had no idea really of what was required from both Mike and I to build a strong marriage. Among other things, I hadn't learnt to cook properly, so I relied on the local butcher to tell me each day how to cook the meat I purchased. He was a patient and friendly guy who gave me different ideas to try.

During our second year of marriage, after some difficulty with becoming pregnant, my doctor sent me for infertility tests at the local Woman's Hospital. It was a training centre for young doctors, so every month I had different examinations and tests done, while a group of awkward-looking young men listened and observed what the qualified doctor was doing. I was rarely spoken to or acknowledged, apart from the initial "hello" and the obligatory name check. This attitude was typical of the 1970s. A nurse said to me, "Leave your dignity at the front door when you come in and collect it again on your way out!"

Eventually, it was decided that I needed to have dye injected into my fallopian tubes to see if they were open for the eggs to come down. I lay on the hospital bed surrounded by technicians and medical staff, who explained what was about to happen and encouraged me to watch a small screen to see the progress of the dye. Unfortunately, my body reacted to the dye and it caused a burning sensation that grew steadily worse as the volume of dye increased. At first, I was gasping and then crying and protesting until finally, I was sobbing, feeling like my abdomen was on fire. After the procedure was finished, I was told to make my way to a side booth, get dressed, and return to work. I was in such agony that they had to carry me into the booth, where I lay for a long time, coming to terms with what had just happened. After a few hours, I hired a taxi cab to take me back to work, where I sat stunned and miserable. My colleagues were kind and supportive, which helped me recover. The silver lining was that I became pregnant soon after the ghastly dye test, for which I was very grateful! In September of 1974, Joshua was born. I was besotted by him, and nicknamed him, 'The Incredible Kid.'

1974 should have been a happy year, as I gave birth to a beautiful baby boy. Instead, a change had taken place in Mike. In my ignorance, I did not realise that just because he had lovely brown eyes and played the guitar well, that did not guarantee a great marriage! Since discovering drugs, Mike was away most weekends partying. Sometimes he insisted that I joined him, even though I had no interest in alcohol or drugs. On one of these occasions, when it became quite late in the evening,

I started feeling very tired. The owner of the house showed me to a room where I could lie down until Mike was ready to take me home. As I began to doze off, I was struck over the head by a heavy object, which thankfully bounced back off and didn't knock me out. I immediately sat up in bed and looked at the man who had just hit me with a glass beer bottle in order to knock me unconscious so he could take advantage of me. I began yelling loudly and ran out into the hallway. People were rushing out of the lounge to see what the commotion was all about. I explained what had just happened and pointed out the man, but then had to dash to the toilet where I began vomiting. My head had a huge swollen egg on it which was understandably painful. Mike, although drunk, could see how distraught I was and quickly took me home. The next day as I walked from the bus to my workplace, I realised that I was walking on a slant across the road. A man helped me back to the sidewalk and after hearing my story he said that I probably had concussion. He called a taxi to take me to the hospital, where I had to put a lead jacket on to protect the baby before having an x-ray. I was told that it was fortunate I had a hard head, because there was no permanent damage. That was the last party I attended for a long time.

Sometimes the party would be at our small cottage, with Mike's friends getting the munchies and devouring all the food they could find. One memorable night, the music was playing so loud that I couldn't get baby Joshua to sleep and had to sit up most of the night rocking him. I was exhausted the next day, hoping his friends would fall asleep or go home and leave me in peace. Mike was also becoming known to the police, who unexpectedly raided our home while I was cooking dinner one evening. I was shocked to see them swarm into our house and begin to search for drugs. One officer told Mike that he needed to rethink what he was doing, as he had a wife and a lovely baby to care for. After searching each room, they left empty-handed and no doubt, frustrated. Mike laughed and showed me where he had hidden a small packet of cannabis in the light shade of the bathroom.

Taking drugs was the start of three years of violence, which escalated as Mike became more addicted. On a Friday night, he would go out with his friends and only return on a Sunday night or Monday morning when he came back to change his clothes and get ready for work. My mind worked overtime during our marriage, searching for ways to stop the violence. But my best plans were ineffectual, as Mike was on a path of pleasure and indulgence which included having a series of affairs. This was a very low time for me. I felt humiliated, trapped, and rejected all over again. His adultery and the violence had gradually robbed me of a sense of security and self-worth. Our marriage was rapidly falling apart.

Around this time, my parent's marriage broke up and to my surprise, my father began to visit me, complaining about being left alone. I felt like his parent; I was always listening, making him cups of tea, and trying to say something appropriate. Soon after, both he and Mum met new partners and their lives went in different directions. I was deeply concerned for my younger siblings who sometimes came to stay with me, but the reality was that my own situation was so overwhelming that I didn't have answers for the mess I was in, let alone any wise advice for someone else.

Meanwhile, things in my home continued to escalate. One day when I asked Mike if he had the money for our rent, he lashed out and hit me across the chest with a large, glass milk bottle. It was very painful. I was so shocked at his actions that I just stared at him. As the beatings increased in frequency and severity I would find myself yelling, in a blind panic, "I love you, I love you!" hoping that this would be enough to stop him, but it had no impact at all. I realised that Mike could injure me badly if I stayed with him. He often hit me around the head and even pounded my head into the wooden window sill in our kitchen. The back of my head would be so badly bruised, that I couldn't brush my hair for days. A neighbour commented one day that she and her husband had been watching through their window as my husband beat me. I asked her "Why didn't you come over and ask for a cup of sugar?" (to interrupt the beating). She looked at me with a questioning frown and replied: "But I didn't need any sugar!" I shook my head in disbelief. Surely human decency dictates that you try to help someone vulnerable, especially if you can see them being abused. In their case, they watched from a safe distance and then carried on with their evening.

The man I was living with was not the gentle, humorous man I had

Right: me - aged 16

*Below: Mum with four
children - I am on the right*

*Right: Jane (right) and
I travelling around
New Zealand*

Left: My Maori Mum and Dad - Terry and April McGregor

Right:
Me, at age 19,
newly married

Mike and I at our wedding

Mike and I with newborn Joshua

Mike and I with baby Joshua - December 1974

Right: Mike entertaining Joshua

1978 (far left - back row) Aranui High School, where I completed my education as an adult student

married. The drugs had turned him into a cold, distant, and cruel person. It felt like we had been caught in a fast-paced, swirling whirlpool. We were sinking deeper and deeper.

When our son Joshua was two years old, he toddled up to me and kicked me in my ankle. I was stunned, but then realised that if I stayed with Mike, Joshua would grow up thinking that abusing women was natural and acceptable. I needed to remove him from this environment, and soon saw an opportunity.

During my pregnancy, Mike had been involved in a serious truck accident, injuring his legs and forcing him to stay in the hospital for several weeks. I was working full-time in the city at an office, so each day at 5 p.m., I walked into the city centre, caught a bus, and began an hour-long trip to see Mike in hospital. After visiting hours, I made the long trek back home to have a quick dinner and fall into bed exhausted. This was my daily pattern for several months.

Two years later when Mike's drug-taking and violent behaviour was becoming too much for me, he received a pay-out of several thousand dollars for the injuries to his legs and to compensate for the time he had spent off work. Since I was entitled to half the settlement, I saw this as a good opportunity for me to make a fresh start for Joshua and myself, so I filed for separation. I was of course very hurt by Mike's behaviour towards me, but grateful to finally be out of the marriage.

Mike was deeply shocked by my leaving and apologised continually for many years, saying that once he realised how much he had hurt me, he vowed to never hit a woman again. Losing his son was also a painful blow, but the truth was that due to the alcohol and drugs he was not responsible enough to care for a little boy.

With great relief, I bought a lovely, brand new, two-bedroom flat in Aranui, where I had grown up. The sense of security and the peace of mind that went with it was wonderful. I no longer spent my nights wondering where Mike was or who he was with, and best of all, I no longer spent my days fearing what he would do to me once he came home.

But there was another side to my new freedom, and the reality was that once again, I was starting out alone. I was not interested in men at all due to years of betrayal, abuse, and pain. It had taken its toll on me and I had thick walls around my heart in an attempt to protect myself. Instead, I concentrated on raising Joshua and landscaping our lovely garden. A friend built a chicken run for the four hens I bought. Each morning, Joshua would run outside and lift the lid to the nesting box In the hope of finding warm eggs. He adored animals but cuddled the hens so much that one was accidentally injured. The most humane thing to do was to wring its neck and bury it in the garden. The next day a neighbour rang me in a panic. She had opened her door when she heard a knock and there stood Joshua with the limp, dirt-covered hen being held high as he asked her if he could show her son the dead bird! I thought it was funny and typical of four-year-old Josh, but she was offended and wanted me to collect him immediately!

My new flat was part of a complex that had eight flats in total. We were a multi-cultural group, comprising of eight Kiwi women, four of whom were married to men from different countries: Greece, India, Ghana, and Japan. A high school friend, Helen, lived with her Ghanaian husband, Francis, in the front flat that I drove past every day. Francis was a flamboyant extrovert who loved entertaining and was very proud of his cooking skills. He frequently invited me to join them for an authentic African meal but I politely refused. I think he was curious about the uptight, sad person that I was, and had a desire to see me relax and enjoy life. Most weekends Helen and Francis's home was filled with many African people that I later learnt were students attending the various universities and colleges around our city. Each time I drove past their flat I saw joyful people dressed in beautifully-coloured African clothing, laughing and dancing together. They looked so happy and free. I envied them because they had created a strong, joyful community where celebrating was a key ingredient.

Life was an absolute mystery to me. Why did some people have a stable marriage, a faithful husband and supportive family, while I seemed to live with constant turmoil, drama, abuse and rejection? I couldn't work out the answer. Even though I was curious about this vibrant group of friendly people, I kept my distance as I needed time alone to heal and to get my bearings on life again.

CHAPTER FIVE
Solomon
1978 – 1980

About a year after I moved into my new flat, I finally began to visit Helen and Francis, meeting some of their African friends in the process. I enjoyed their relaxed, light-hearted attitudes and found they were, for the most part, kind people who faced all sorts of challenges as a minority in my country. One of their friends was Solomon, a Zimbabwean man who was studying engineering at Canterbury University. He had a great sense of humour and was kind, gentle, and very wise. Solomon befriended me and would patiently listen as I shared some of the challenges I was having raising my son on my own. He was a good listener and very patient as I struggled to express myself. Feeling insecure and vulnerable made it difficult for me to be open with him, but I enjoyed having someone to talk with. Solomon gave me different ideas to try for situations where I was feeling overwhelmed and discouraged. I was finding it difficult raising a high energy lad on my own and I was grateful for Solomon's input, which began making a noticeable difference in Josh's behaviour.

For a year, Solomon and I rang each other to share our dreams, hopes and daily struggles. After that year of being friends, he asked me if I would go out with him on a date, but I declined. He bluntly said, "You don't think I am good-looking, do you?" I was shocked! That was exactly what I thought, but I felt guilty for judging him on his looks, so I denied it. I was averse to having a relationship with Solomon because he was not very good-looking (I secretly thought he looked like a short professor) but also because he was a black African (he was conspicuous!). I had noticed that people would stare at us when we were out in public together, mainly because there were few black Africans in my city at that time, and this made me very uncomfortable. I was not secure enough to handle being an object of curiosity and imagined people were looking down at me. Eventually, I agreed to go on a date and after a while, I realised that I loved this caring, funny, wise man, so I stopped worrying about people staring at us and simply enjoyed being loved and cared for. As Solomon and I enjoyed our newfound relationship and began making plans about our future, optimism slowly returned to my life. This was the person to whom I was special, the person for whom I had been searching for so many years.

Solomon spoke at length about his beautiful country, Zimbabwe, which he intended returning to after he gained his degree. He planned to help his nation once independence was achieved. Zimbabwe was a landlocked nation of 7.5 million people at that time, where a total of sixteen languages were spoken, including English. At that time, though,

Zimbabwe was known as Southern Rhodesia, a long-time British colony deeply divided on racial lines. In 1961, Ian Smith, a former fighter pilot during the Second World War, founded The Rhodesian Front, a political party which attracted the support of white supremacists. Smith was an ardent advocate of white rule, and in 1962 his party won the election. In 1964, Smith became the Prime Minister, and in November 1965, he declared Southern Rhodesia's independence from Great Britain. However, this independence was not formally recognised and as a result, the United Nations Security Council imposed economic sanctions on Smith's government. Smith reacted by severing all ties with the Commonwealth.

For fifteen years, war raged between Zimbabwean guerrilla forces, led by Joshua Nkomo and Robert Mugabe, against Ian Smith's government, who were committed to keeping tight control of the nation they considered to be their own. In terms of human dignity, the cost of enforced white rule for the local Shona and Ndebele peoples was very high. They were second class citizens in their nation. No longer free to move around, they were required to carry official pass documents just to travel from their overcrowded townships to their workplaces, which included luxurious suburbs where the white people lived.

Many local Africans received only a basic education and had limited choices as to where they worked. Many worked as maids, cooks, gardeners, childminders, labourers and miners, all receiving a pittance of a wage. Living all my life in peaceful New Zealand, I could not imagine the lifestyle Solomon described to me. He shared many stories of injustice and deprivation that had horribly impacted his family and community. At the beginning of 1980, the Zimbabwean students were becoming more optimistic and expectant that liberation from white rule was about to happen.

Finally, in mid-1980 a peace agreement establishing sovereignty for black Zimbabweans was created. Colonialism was over. Zimbabwe, rich in minerals and agriculture—the breadbasket of Africa—would be ruled by its indigenous people, the rightful owners of the land and their own destinies. The first president was Robert Mugabe, a highly educated lawyer of whom everyone had high expectations. Solomon and his friends were jubilant and celebrated with laughter, dancing and also tears as they remembered all their friends and family who had been killed during the fifteen years of war.

Some of the things I loved about Solomon were his wisdom and sense of humour. For example, he had an interesting way of helping me quit smoking. I had been smoking about thirty cigarettes a day for eight years and was concerned about my health, but lacked the willpower to overcome the habit. One day Solomon said to me, "Chris, I bet you can't give up that filthy habit." I decided to prove him wrong. I set up a strategy whereby I rang my friends who smoked and told them not to visit me for a week. I then stopped drinking coffee, as it is a stimulant, and was also usually accompanied by a smoke. Each day that I managed without one, I coloured the date on my calendar in bright red crayon. Gradually the red line grew and after six days I announced to everyone that I had given up smoking. When I told Solomon he grinned and said, "Good girl, I knew you could do it!" He had deliberately goaded me, knowing I would rise to the challenge. This accomplishment gave me a strong sense of empowerment and encouraged me to begin planning my next big goal.

For some time, I had been contemplating completing my education that had been interrupted in my sixteenth year. The government had introduced a scheme whereby adult students could return to a high school of their choice to attend classes and sit for their School Certificate or University Entrance exams. I decided to apply to my old high school in Aranui, and for a year I attended daily classes with teenage students, happily completing my studies. A friend took care of Joshua, and without the tensions of my childhood life, I thoroughly enjoyed myself and flourished. The teenage students were friendly and naturally curious about me returning to school. Once again I became passionate about English literature, my favourite subject, and worked hard to pass the exams. It was exciting to receive a letter stating I had passed each subject and had qualified to enroll for university. Solomon was thrilled for me and helped me to choose some subjects for the coming year: Education, Sociology and Psychology. I was like a sponge attending all the lectures and reading as much on each topic as I could. A new world had opened up to me. The whole atmosphere of the university buzzed with purpose and possibilities. What a pleasure to learn so much and to be with fascinating people every day.

Returning to school also taught me a great life lesson: to not see myself as a victim or to live with a sense of defeat, but to find a way to achieve my goals. As an adult, I was determined to complete my high school education, and by doing so at age twenty-five I reclaimed something of great value that was stolen from me in my teens. To go on to university was even more momentous. No one in my family had ever been to university. The sense of achievement was so enormous that I felt empowered in a way I had never experienced before. My future now seemed filled with more possibilities than I had ever imagined. Life was wonderful and getting better by the day!

Because Solomon was studying full-time at University, we only saw each other on weekends. Initially, he had been very supportive and encouraging, but to my great disappointment I began to notice signs of anger and manipulation. I loved Solomon deeply but, after years of unhappiness in my previous marriage, I was not prepared for a repeat of that experience. I had become Intolerant to anger and abuse, so I began to contemplate ending our relationship.

In the midst of this season, I received a devastating phone call from a younger McGregor sister telling me that my Maori Dad had died in a car accident. My heart was broken. I quickly packed some necessities and then began the long drive up to Waitotara with Joshua.

In Maori culture, when someone dies, a *tangi* is held in honour of the deceased person. A huge marquee stood on the grounds of Ihupuku Pa, providing a sleeping place for families and friends arriving from all over New Zealand. Dad lay in a coffin in a smaller *whare*, with Mum and a smaller group sleeping near Dad. We were all in shock at his sudden passing, with many tears being shed during the *tangi* service. Mum looked bereft and so alone without her life-long companion.

On the third day, I was feeling unwell, so a close friend took me to her doctor. He examined me and asked a few questions, and then shocked me by announcing that I was three months pregnant. No way! This couldn't be true. I had struggled previously with infertility which resulted in my having to endure unpleasant monthly tests at the Christchurch Women's Hospital for a year before becoming pregnant with Joshua. The specialist had informed me that it was unlikely I would have another child. I had believed him, but was now being told I was about to become a mother again!

My mind was in turmoil, trying to process Dad's death and then this unexpected news added to it. I spent a few days with Mum after the funeral, then headed back to Christchurch, knowing I had some serious decisions to make.

I had decided to break up with Solomon. The thought that I would be a mother of two children with two different fathers was unsettling enough, let alone the knowledge that I would once again raise a child alone. On my return to Christchurch, I worried about my situation day and night, concerned I was about to make some big mistakes that I might regret afterwards.

About six days later Solomon rang and asked when I had arrived back. He was shocked when he learnt I had not contacted him upon my arrival. He said he was coming over immediately, but I asked him not to. I knew he was determined to find out what was happening, so I waited with trepidation, knowing I was about to end our relationship. I knew he would not be happy, but worried he could possibly become angry at me. A taxi cab arrived and Solomon rushed inside, looking quite anxious. I explained that I was pregnant with his baby and that we were finished due to his controlling behaviour. He looked crestfallen and asked me to reconsider and then said, "I knew that if you had an opportunity to spend time away from me, you would realise that I had been manipulating you." His admission stunned me because it meant his behaviour was calculated and intentional. His statement only strengthened my resolve to end something that I was no longer feeling peaceful or happy about. When I refused to reconsider he became quite emotional and said, "In all my life I never thought I would trust a white person, let alone love one, and I love you."

I felt awful as I saw the reaction my unexpected news had created. I was also emotional as this was the man I had expected to marry and spend the rest of my life with. It was harder than I had thought it would be, but I had lost trust in him and was afraid of being hurt again. Deep down I knew I was not secure enough to navigate this type of behaviour, which would of course surface again if we got back together. I did not waiver in my decision and our relationship ended that night.

As university was about to start again, I chose three subjects for the second year and began to attend classes. To my dismay, as a side effect of the pregnancy, my mind felt like mush and no matter how many times I read a page, nothing stuck. It was with deep regret that I met with the Dean and resigned from my studies, hoping I would resume them after the baby was born.

As the weeks passed, I became lonely and anxious about my future. I was desperately seeking answers, but not finding any. Then an idea began to form that seemed wise to me: I would hand back the ownership of my flat to the State Housing Corporation and go off in search of God! Galvanised by this adventurous plan I began disposing of our furniture and possessions and soon headed off up the coastal road, taking the overnight ferry across to the North Island. I reasoned that if I could find a small place to live, where no one knew me, then surely God would meet with me. If this happened, then I would have a better life than all the brokenness and turmoil that had accompanied me so far.

I was now four and a half months pregnant with a six-year-old son in the backseat of the car, surrounded by his toys, our blankets, pots and pans. At Wellington city, I stopped in to see Mike's parents and discovered his mother had just had a big operation, so we stayed with them for a week while I took care of her and her home.

As I continued driving up the coast, stopping at each place that appealed, I was repeatedly told there were no cottages or flats available to rent. My quest to find God was not as easy as I initially thought it would be! With a confused and sad heart, I finally reached Waitotara. I briefly considered setting up home there, but after talking it over with my Maori sisters they encouraged me to return to Christchurch. I had been so sure that God would reveal Himself to me on the journey, but I now had to admit defeat.

As I drove back down the coast, with travel-weary Joshua and a growing tummy, I felt embarrassed that I would soon be meeting up with my biological family and friends, all of whom I had farewelled only a few weeks before. My biggest concern, of course, was that we no longer had a home to which to return. Unbeknownst to me, God had been watching my heartfelt search for Him and had already provided for our every need.

When I rang my sister Sophie, she gave me the unexpected news that I could have her flat as she was about to move into a rental home. The timing was absolutely perfect! I was relieved because I was five months pregnant and feeling drained from all the travelling and many disappointments. I knew Joshua was longing to be settled and near his beloved Nana again. Thankfully the flat was ready for us to move into immediately, but even so, I couldn't help comparing the old building to our lovely new flat I had so easily given up.

Feeling weary and vulnerable, I rang Solomon to tell him we had returned. He was delighted and biked over in the cold to see us. I could see the concern in his eyes as I related the details of our trip. As the days passed and Josh began attending a local primary school, my need to connect with God became stronger. The feelings of vulnerability and aloneness grew as I contemplated the mess I had made of my life up to this point.

Meanwhile, my sister Sophie had met several Christians living close to her and had begun attending a church called Faith Family. Whenever I visited her she would speak to me about her new life with God and I could not deny the deep peace she now had. Her friends were caring people who opened their homes to new converts and those in need of food or a place to stay. It was a vibrant, caring community, with many recovering drug addicts or people who had been in prison. I resisted Sophie's efforts to get me involved and would leave abruptly, as I was convinced that church was just for old people or those who couldn't find a partner. I wasn't that desperate!

God smiled. He knew me better than I knew myself.

Marty and Talma Biddle from Faith Family, Aranui / Wainoni

CHAPTER SIX

Surrender

MARCH 1980

When I was 27 I surrendered my life to the Lord, even though I didn't know what I was doing. One evening, after a week of stress and worry, everything became too much for me. My head felt like it would explode with all the agonizing I had been doing. I began to bang my head on a kitchen cupboard to try and ease the desperate anguish in my mind. By now I was almost six months pregnant and was not feeling confident about being able to care for six-year-old Joshua as well as a new baby. I knew I couldn't carry on like this. It wasn't healthy for any of us. After assessing my situation, I realised that I needed help. I thought, "I need help from either a man or God. I am sick of men, so I will give God a go." Decision made! Feeling calmer, I knelt on the lounge floor (because I believed you needed to kneel when you talked to God) and said with desperation, "I am going to give you a shot at my life, but you better prove yourself!" I stood up without much expectation and began waiting to see if God had heard my prayer. The big dilemma for me was whether or not God was real, and if he was, would He communicate personally with me?

As I waited, I decided I had to be practical, so I found a telephone book for our city and began looking for all the churches that were close to us. As I prepared a list with the addresses and service times, I decided that the Salvation Army would be the first one I would visit, believing that they put their money where their mouth was. I was impressed by their community welfare projects, like feeding the poor and helping to rehabilitate alcoholics.

That weekend, I attended a Sunday service at the Salvation Army in Linwood. Before I entered the church building, I sat in the car with Josh and said to God, "Okay God, I'm going in now, and someone will have to be really friendly to me before I will believe that you exist."

As a child, I attended an Anglican church for a short while, but this was very different in every way. I loved the sense of order, with everyone wearing a smart military-style uniform and the structured service, which included items from the brass band, scriptures read aloud, and a short message. Everything had military terms, in keeping with the theme of an army. This amused and fascinated me. After the meeting, a slim older woman wearing high heels came tottering towards me. She enthusiastically expressed both kindness and concern as she wrapped her arms around me, and said how wonderful it was that we had come to visit them that morning. Then she whispered, as she looked at my swollen abdomen, "We have thrift shops with good quality affordable baby clothes." With a huge smile, she moved on to greet someone else. I said to the Lord, "That was a good start, but it's not enough, I need more!"

The Captain and his wife were standing by the front door as we left, shaking hands and saying goodbye to each person filing out. I felt very self-conscious and would have avoided them, but I was in a queue and my turn was rapidly coming up to meet this couple. To my surprise, Enid, the Captain's wife, invited me for tea the next day.

When I arrived, she welcomed me warmly and ushered me into their lounge. In a sensitive manner, she asked about the baby. I told her that the father was a foreigner, from Africa. I expected her to look a bit shocked but instead, she was genuinely interested and asked me what his home country was. When I replied it was Zimbabwe, she looked delighted and told me that they had just returned to New Zealand after ministering in Zimbabwe for four years! She then began showing me their Zimbabwean sandstone carvings standing on the bookcase. I was stunned. Of all the churches in my area that I had chosen to visit, the first one had leaders who had been missionaries in Solomon's country. This clinched it for me! God really did exist and He was interested in me. He had just done something quite extraordinary to prove Himself to me, just as I had requested.

Straight away, Enid and I bonded. She took me under her wing and had me working with her each Friday in the thrift shop. When we visited elderly people, Enid would ask me to give my testimony about how I came to know God. This was my first experience of speaking to strangers about my faith and I found I enjoyed it immensely.

At the thrift shop, I saw the abundance of clothing and bedding and suggested to Enid that we could fill big, heavy-duty paper sacks with clothing and send them to Solomon's mother in Zimbabwe. From corresponding with her regularly, I knew she would enjoy distributing the items to those in need in her community; their need was much greater than ours! Enid agreed to my idea and we began choosing the best items to fill each bag. Once they were sealed and addressed, I prayed for their safe arrival before posting each one. Every single bag we sent arrived safely, which was amazing, considering the sacks were just strong paper. On Monday mornings, the volunteers would notice the shelves were considerably thinned out and assumed Enid and I had sold large quantities of clothing on Friday. She never enlightened them as to their true destination! I loved Enid deeply, as she treated me with kindness and respect.

At her prompting, after some training, I began to teach Bible in School classes each week at local primary schools. For half an hour, I led the children in a few short choruses, then told a Bible story with a flannel board that had different scenes and characters to illustrate the story.

Josh and I in the car with our cat on our journey to 'find God'.

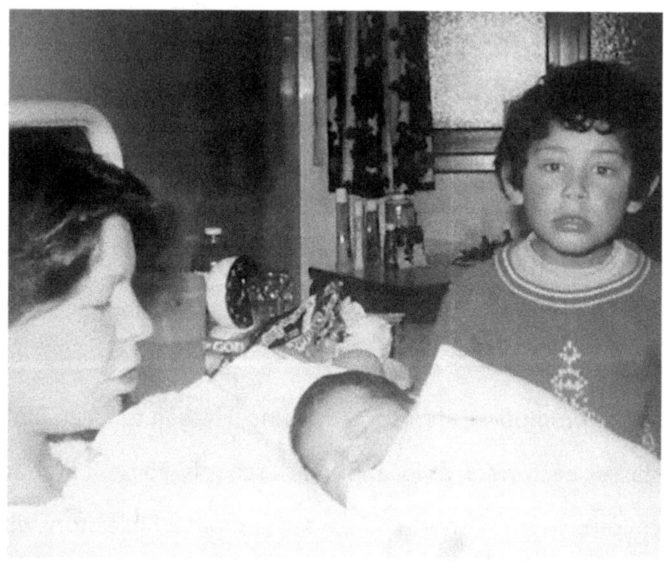

With newborn Eli and 6 year old Josh, I am 27 years old

After teaching the timeless truths found in the Bible, I would end with a memory verse and a closing prayer. I loved teaching the children so much that I went on to teach Bible in Schools for ten years, sometimes teaching several classes a week.

As God began revealing more of his character and His presence to me, I realised that he was the one who had been gently whispering to me for years, "You are special." I could finally stop searching for that elusive person; I had found Him.

However, deep in my heart, I was hopeful that there would be a kind steady man for me and my children in the future. I felt that they needed a father. So one day I said to God, "I just want an ordinary life, with an ordinary man. I don't want any more drama or anything unusual to happen again." I then thanked Him, believing He would do exactly what I had requested. Little did I know that an ordinary life was not part of the calling God had for my life.

As I began to read my new Bible, I was thrilled with all the promises I discovered. My heavenly father was generous, kind, and protective. To my surprise, I learnt that God loves to communicate, sometimes in interesting ways, and often through His word. He was not fazed by how broken and distrusting I was. In fact, He proved Himself to me many times, reassuring me that He was committed to caring and providing for me and the children. On two separate occasions, he even called out my name audibly when I was alone in my home. I felt in awe of my Heavenly Father proving His existence to me this way! I loved God and was determined to obey whatever He asked me to do.

While I read the New Testament, I saw that Jesus was baptised in water by his cousin John. I decided that if it was important to Jesus, then I needed to follow his example. Because the Salvation Army didn't water baptise believers, I asked some of my new friends to accompany me to our local beach and baptise me there. It was a powerful spiritual experience. When I came up out of the water, I truly felt like a new person with a fresh future awaiting me.

Reading the stories of people who either followed God's instructions or rebelled and did their own thing, I discovered that all choices had consequences and were a key element in the outcome of each person's life. Realising this, I was determined to make better decisions in the future, ones that pleased God. In this way, I was trusting that my life and the lives of my children would be free of all the turmoil we had experienced up to this point. After a lifetime of feeling starved of connection, belonging, and guidance, I felt secure, purposeful, and excited about the future.

In July 1980 I gave birth to a healthy baby boy, Eli, at the Salvation Army hospital. During Eli's birth, I had lost a considerable amount of blood because the young, inexperienced doctor had accidentally cut me near a vein. For days I felt quite faint whenever I stood up for any length of time. I stayed in the hospital for ten days while I recovered and gained my strength back. The matron was nurturing and kind to me, spending hours listening and giving me wise motherly advice. I was conflicted because I still loved Solomon. I knew that if he surrendered his life to God and dealt with his anger, we could probably continue with our relationship. That way, I would have someone to help me raise the boys and we would be a complete family unit. Because he wasn't showing any interest in coming to church, I prayed constantly for a change in his heart.

During this emotional time, I became upset one evening, as Solomon had said he was going to visit, but he hadn't. The matron was concerned and rang the doctor, asking if he would come to see me. To my surprise, that evening, when I was red-eyed and my face was swollen from crying, the young doctor appeared in my room in full evening dress! He was about to take his wife out when the matron called him. To his credit, he put my needs first and sat beside me as I poured out my tale of woe. He replied with a statement I never forgot, "Christine, don't listen to what a man says to you. Look at his actions." I was very grateful for the care I received from both the matron and the doctor. On my last day, the matron handed me her treasured book of Helen Steiner Rice poems, hoping they would bring me comfort in the years ahead, which they did.

After Eli was born, Enid and her family moved out of the large older style house they had been renting and asked me if I wanted it. I was keen to exchange the dark, pokey little flat we had been renting for a lovely big house. While we lived there, Enid would sometimes ask me to help people who were struggling in their family relationships. One such person was a beautiful young Filipino lady, Joy. When she was a teenager living with her parents in the Philippines she began corresponding with an older man in New Zealand. Joy thought it was a bit of fun to write to him, pretending she was romantically interested in him. He often sent Joy money, which she and her boyfriend happily spent. However, it all backfired when he arrived at her parent's home, introducing himself as Joy's fiancé. To her shock and dismay, her parents insisted that Joy marry him. Her broken-hearted boyfriend watched the ceremony from a distance. On arriving in Christchurch, Joy discovered that her elderly "sugar daddy" was just an ordinary old man, living on a limited pension in a cold, isolated caravan. Within weeks she was depressed and, in desperation, contacted the Salvation Army looking for help. I was asked to meet with Joy and support her while she decided what to do. In a short space of time, she had met a young man and begun a new relationship.

Three people came to live with us, for a short while, so they could sort their lives out and then move on. Each person had deep issues that prevented them from relating well to others. I learnt a great deal in my efforts to help each one of them.

In 1981, I began attending my sister Sophie's church in the evenings. Many of the church members were recovering drug addicts, alcoholics, gang members, or men who had spent time in prison. Faith Family Fellowship was a warm, welcoming gathering with people who worshipped in an uninhibited way. They were zealous about their newfound faith. I was fascinated by how different they were to the Salvation Army that I had been attending for a year. The people dressed casually, the worship was enthusiastic and loud, and people invited newcomers to a meal or to stay if they were homeless. Over time, I met several of Sophie's friends and was impressed with their dedication and desire to help one another. The leaders, George and Wyn Ehau—a patient, warm, mature Maori couple—were like parents to many people who had never known acceptance and encouragement. They thrived in this environment.

Sophie explained to me the importance of being filled with the Holy Spirit, but that just seemed a bit extreme to me, so I dismissed this as being unimportant. I was content with having a wonderful heavenly Father who loved me and getting to know Jesus my saviour who had made it possible for me to have a relationship with God. Jesus was my role model and inspiration. This all changed one Sunday night during ministry time when I experienced deliverance in a powerful way and could no longer deny the power of the Holy Spirit. I finally felt free of the hurt and unforgiveness that had plagued me for years.

A key figure in my life at that time was a man called Marty Biddle, who was also a member of Faith Family. He was a Maori man who was an ex-gang leader. Marty was a mature Christian man who was running a home, close to Sophie's, for young men who needed nurturing and rehabilitation. I would often visit Marty at his home, drinking endless cups of tea from a battered old metal teapot that had a saucer on top instead of a lid, while Eli slept in his pram. I had so many questions about God, life, and the teachings in the Bible. Marty patiently answered all my questions, often with a smile, probably because I was so intense and impatient for change to happen quickly! At times he was quite blunt with me when he needed to be because I had a victim mentality and Marty would challenge me to take responsibility in different areas.

With his help, I grew in my understanding of following God. He also encouraged me to ask God to be baptised in the Holy Spirit and to speak in tongues. This didn't appeal to me at all; it just sounded really strange. One evening while I was visiting some of the new believers from Faith Family, the topic of conversation was about being filled with the Holy Spirit and speaking in tongues. I listened to each of them and then firmly stated the reason why I didn't need to seek this experience. Looking over at Marty who was sitting nearby, I saw he had a big grin on his face. This annoyed me. I was listening to some of the young folk praying out loud when, suddenly, I burst out in a very loud voice with a language that I didn't recognise. This outburst was so intense that the words were rushing out. I felt embarrassed as I was making quite a noise and it was late at night. I had been resisting the Holy Spirit for so long that when I finally began to speak in tongues, it came whooshing out with such force and intensity that it surprised me and no doubt, everyone else in the room. I was absolutely amazed but had a wonderful sense of being utterly liberated. Marty was laughing at this sudden turn of events after my declarations of disinterest in speaking in tongues. I also saw the funny side of this later on and we laughed together.

During my season at Faith Family, God was busy freeing me of deep things that had been hindering me for a long time. It was wonderful also to see my younger sister Sophie gradually change into a happy, confident, and secure person.

CHAPTER SEVEN
God Calling
1980 – 1983

While I was still at the Salvation Army church, I met a seventeen-year-old university student named Ruth. Ruth lived one street away from me after I moved into the Captain and Enid's old house, and quickly became my closest friend. She often came to help with Joshua and Eli after school and shared many meals with us in our home. She was passionate about her faith and encouraged me a lot when I was a new believer. Most importantly, God used her to guide my early understanding and explain what my life could look like if I served God. Of course, being a mother was my priority, but I yearned to serve God beyond my home. Ruth began lending me books about the lives of famous missionaries who had left their home country to serve God in quite primitive settings, and I loved to read them.

I was astounded at the story of Mary Slessor, for example, who came from a very poor and abusive background in Scotland. She left everything that was familiar to her and travelled to Calabar, Nigeria in the mid-1800s. Once in Nigeria she learned the local Efik language and began to educate local children. Because of her boldness and sincerity, Mary quickly gained the trust of locals, including the chiefs of her region. After some time she was given permission to share the gospel freely. Mary also promoted women's rights. It was at a time when a woman was beaten if she gave birth to twins, as people believed multiple births were caused by evil spirits. The babies of multiple births were put into the jungle for wild animals to eat, but Mary rescued many of these twins. It was not easy to care for them all and at one time she had to wrap the babies in newspaper, as she had run out of donated clothes and blankets.

Mary's work and heart for women and children brought major changes to laws that had been created out of superstition and fear. She helped to create a more humane society for the most vulnerable. Today, there are still many statues honouring her in Calabar, Nigeria. Several schools, roads, and churches have also been named after her. I became excited at what God had accomplished with her surrendered life. So many people trapped in darkness, deception, and pain were set free.

Another book Ruth lent me was the story of Amy Carmichael. She was a lovely little girl who always wanted blue eyes like her mother. One night Amy prayed and asked God to change her eyes from brown to blue. She was disappointed when she woke up and saw in the mirror that her eyes were still the same colour. Amy felt confused, believing God had not answered her prayer. However, some years later when Amy went to

India, she realised because she had brown eyes, she was able to dress in the local costume of a sari and disguise herself as an Indian. In this way, she gained access to little children who had been sold or given to work in the temples. For years Amy rescued hundreds of children from Hindu temples where they were suffering all kinds of abuse.

The temple workers nicknamed her "Missie child catcher." Even though she was portrayed as a terrible person, the abused children ran away from the temple to her home. The first girl who arrived at her front door showed Amy the burn marks on the palms of her little hands. Amy shared with her the story of a Saviour who also had been injured on the palms of his hands as he was nailed to the cross. For over 50 years Amy rescued many children. She founded the Dohnavur Fellowship, an organization still running today, and wrote forty books. She is famous for her total dedication to a very difficult calling.

As my friend Ruth continued to bring me missions books, I grew to believe that this was the "normal" Christian life that God had planned for each of us. All the books I read impacted my worldview and understanding of what was possible if Christians stepped outside of their comfort zones, trusted God, and took a few risks. One of God's many promises to us is that He will "never leave us or forsake us." No matter where we go, He will always be with us, leading the way. I eagerly awaited His instructions for me!

I had an extraordinary experience one day while I was doing something very ordinary. As I hung out Eli's cloth nappies on the clothesline in the backyard, three scenes suddenly appeared in front of my eyes. I only remember two. One was of an aerial shot of an island that looked like a big rock, surrounded by sea. Immediately, I was aware that I would be flying somewhere. The second scene was of a very wide and beautiful waterfall. In my spirit, I knew I was going overseas. I shouted and ran inside to tell Ruth what I had just seen. We were both amazed at God giving me a vision, especially while I was doing my household chores. I had imagined that people only saw visions while they were praying! As we speculated what the different pictures could mean, I asked God to reveal where the waterfall was.

Several weeks later, I received a letter from Solomon's family, with whom I had stayed in touch. I was stunned to see that one of the stamps had a picture of the exact waterfall that was in my vision. It was Victoria Falls which was on the border of Zimbabwe and Zambia. This confused me at first as I had asked God to just let me settle down with an ordinary man in New Zealand and to have an ordinary life with my sons. Instead, He was showing me that my future lay in Zimbabwe. I was astonished. But I was also excited; I had never travelled outside New Zealand, and this possibility absolutely thrilled me.

My mind was abuzz with all the variety of work I might be able to do in Africa. In order to travel there I would need passports for myself and Eli.

Josh had his issued the year before when he visited his dad in Australia. I immediately applied for Eli's and my passports, knowing they were the first step in this exciting plan. I was convinced that God had given me the vision to prepare me for our imminent departure to Africa, so I drove to a local travel agency to get our tickets. Full of faith, I met with the agent who was also the owner. I told him about the vision from God, and then confidently asked him to book tickets for the boys and me to Zimbabwe. When he asked if I had the money to pay for them, I was surprised and a little disappointed, as he was a Christian and I fully expected that he should have been aware that God would supply the ticket money. He was silent as I replied that God would supply all we needed.

At this point, he called in his young receptionist and sent her out to buy morning tea for us. Thankfully, he was a wise, kind man who didn't react when, after asking me what I intended to do in Zimbabwe, I replied, "I don't know, but I trust God to show me." By now I was beginning to sense that something was not quite right. I was starting to feel self-conscious and a little uneasy. To this man's credit, he did not belittle or embarrass me. In fact, he treated me with respect and paid attention as I spoke. Then in a fatherly manner, he gently encouraged me to wait until I had the money to book the flights. I thanked him for his time and advice and drove back home, feeling mystified that everything hadn't been settled as easily as I had been imagining. God had given me a very clear vision. I was keen to go. So why didn't it happen? As a young

Christian, I still had a great deal to learn!

To my growing dismay, it took ten long years before God opened the doors for us to reach Africa. An important lesson I learned through this experience was that God often gives us a glimpse of what is ahead, but we need to wait until the time of release. My impatience caused me much frustration and confusion for many years until I learned to release the vision and my heart's desire back into His capable hands. "Very truly I tell you, unless a kernel of wheat falls to the ground and dies, it remains only a single seed. But if it dies, it produces many seeds" (John 12:24, NIV).

During this time, an Elim pastor rang me one day to request a room for a young lady who was coming from Blenheim to work in Christchurch. Her parents had asked him to help her get settled, but the accommodation he had arranged had fallen through. Somehow my name was mentioned and a few days later a lovely young lady called Carolyn came to stay with us. She was a caring person who helped me with the boys. I was grateful to have a responsible, self-contained person for company.

Carolyn's mother, Laura, and her brother later came to visit us and, no doubt, to check out with whom she was living. Laura and I clicked immediately. She was a positive person with a great sense of humour and a deep trust in God. Neither of us knew that God had organized the change in Carolyn's accommodation. While Carolyn only lived with us for a year, her parents Laura and Bob were to become key people in our lives. In fact, forty years later, I still consider Laura to be one of my closest friends.

After being at Faith Family for a year, and knowing I was heading out to Africa at some stage to do mission work, I began to hunger to know more and to be prepared for what was ahead. A local Assembly of God church was running a Bible school during the week so I decided to attend this church regularly but at the same time, I visited Faith Family and remained in close contact with the folks there.

Around that time, Sophie told me that Marty had left the fellowship and had moved to Invercargill, which was at the very bottom of the South Island. Apparently, he was living with a group of young men and was out of touch with some of his former friends in Christchurch. Marty had been very special to me, a mentor in my early days of establishing my faith. I could not bear the thought of him living without a close relationship with God.

After praying about his situation, I decided that I would drive to Invercargill and spend a few days with him and his friends. My desire was that he would come back to the Lord. The major hitch to this plan was that I didn't have any money for the necessary fuel or accommodation on the way south. The answer, of course, was to sell something. Realising that my engagement and wedding rings from my marriage to Mike were of no use to me, I took them into a second-hand dealer in the city. I felt that Marty's need was greater, and I had a sense of urgency about this trip. Once I had enough cash for the journey I rang Marty to tell him that Eli and I were coming to stay for a few days. I don't know what he thought about this idea, but he was too well-mannered to tell me to mind my own business and to stay home!

Ruth looked after Joshua and our home while I set off with Eli. He slept in his carrycot on the back seat of my sturdy little Anglia car. We stopped in Dunedin for the night and then continued the journey, arriving in Invercargill the next afternoon. Marty looked awkward initially as he greeted me, but then showed me to my room, where he had thoughtfully nailed together a cot that he had found in the garage. I didn't feel it was my place to tell him that you normally used screws to put a cot together, so you could dismantle it afterwards. After a short nap, I joined the men for dinner. They were all intrigued to see a woman with a toddler suddenly appearing in their midst!

I felt that the best thing I could do during my stay was to make myself useful by tidying up the place a bit and cooking an evening meal for everyone. When Marty and the young men returned from work the next day and sat down for dinner, I asked them to hold hands while I said grace. They were respectful and did so, much to Marty's amusement, I am sure. I was definitely a woman on a mission! For three days I pottered around and prayed with intensity for Marty's situation. I didn't want to pry by asking him a lot of questions. Instead, I hoped that God would break through the walls around his heart and bring restoration to whatever area had been hurt. I was learning that when we are hurt, the enemy of our soul often plants a lie in our mind, which then causes a separation between us and God. Loss of trust usually accompanies hurt.

On my last evening, Marty and I were sitting in the lounge alone, so I took the opportunity to ask him some theological questions. He got up, went to his room, and came back with a very dusty Bible, which he quickly wiped. Marty opened it up slowly, looking at it as one looks at a long lost friend. He then began to explain what different passages meant and answered my questions in his typically patient way. We had a short conversation and then I excused myself to get ready for the long journey the next morning.

I was up bright and early packing the car and feeding Eli before we set off for home. Marty came into the kitchen and said to me that he had been up all night reading the Word. I was so grateful to God when Marty told me He had reconnected with his precious Heavenly Father; this had been the purpose of my impulsive journey. He looked so much more relaxed and at peace with himself. Marty surprised me by asking for my car keys; he wanted to fill the car with fuel. I was grateful for his sensitivity and generosity.

Left: Josh, me and Eli

Above: Me and Eli (2 years old)

Left: Ruth Robertson, me and the boys, Christchurch 1982

As I drove up the coast, I felt incredibly grateful to God for rescuing my dear friend Marty. Sometime later he returned to Christchurch and continued ministering to young people. Marty met and married a beautiful Australian lady, Talma. I was thrilled for him. Marty had spent many years caring for many other people and now it was his turn to be loved and to enjoy some companionship.

Back at home, I was like a thirsty sponge in the Bible school and soaked up all the wonderful teaching. As a budding missionary, I needed to be trained and equipped, and the school was giving me a foundation. Therefore, I was quite shocked during one service when our new Australian pastor stated that divorced people could not have any leadership roles or minister publicly. I knew at this point that I wouldn't be staying there very long! God had created me equal to everyone else. He knew I was divorced, and yet He had put this calling on my life. No one was going to tell me that I had to sit in a pew for the next forty years as an observer instead of serving God, wherever He wanted to send me.

Soon after this enlightening sermon, I was enthusiastically worshiping one Sunday evening when I distinctly heard the words in my spirit: Go to Blenheim. I was startled, but confident that this was God speaking to me. I tapped my friend Ruth on the shoulder and said, "God has just told me to move to Blenheim."

Naturally, she looked a bit stunned, but Ruth was used to me making bold statements after hearing from God. Ruth and I had a unique relationship because even though she was only nineteen and I was twenty-nine, we had a very close, supportive relationship. My family were naturally shocked when I announced to them that we were moving to Blenheim. They felt it was too sudden for such a big decision, and suggested that I meet with the pastors to pray about the move and to seek confirmation. I couldn't understand this advice. I had a simple relationship with God; if I felt He was telling me to do something, then I quickly did it. Wow, did I have some interesting adventures and experiences! Regardless, I am sure He enjoyed the enthusiasm and deep trust of this young Christian called Christine who lived to please her Heavenly Father.

Looking Back

An important lesson on timing and visions:

After waiting for some time for a door to open into a new season, it is tempting to rush ahead once we see the first signs of movement. But we need to stay patient; God's timing is so different from ours and He truly does know best.

Chapter Eight

Transformation

As a young adult, I felt I was a failure and of low worth because of social titles that I allowed to define me. In New Zealand in the 1970s and '80s, there was a negative stigma towards anyone who was a "solo Mum." Reading my Bible each day and listening to messages on Sundays at church, I learned the truth of who I was in God's eyes. Thankfully the label of "solo Mum" stopped defining me. Gradually my security and identity came from God alone.

I began reading the Bible from the first book, Genesis, and continued until I had finished the last book, Revelations. I highlighted all the promises in green. As I read God's word, my views about life, myself, family, and God steadily changed.

A key verse, Romans 12:2, explains this process as being *transformed by the renewing of your mind* (NIV). As a child and then an adult, we develop specific pathways of thinking that become established as truth to us. These truths then regulate much of our thinking and strongly influence the choices we make. Repetitive thoughts and actions, in turn, create strong pathways of which we are not even aware.

I learned about this aspect of the brain when I attended a seminar by Sy Rogers, a man who spent many years living as a woman. He showed us a photo of himself when he was a secretary. He was wearing a dress, had his hair in a big bouffant hairstyle, and makeup on his face. Just as Sy was about to have an operation to help him in his quest to further transform into a woman, he came to know God. He was spared much pain, additional confusion, and depression. Sy had to unlearn female behaviour as he embraced his male identity. He began researching the brain and learnt how each person's pathways of thought and behaviour are created. For decades Sy dedicated his life to helping gay people who want to leave this lifestyle. With his newfound knowledge, he gave them tools to interrupt the old familiar pathways and to lay down new tracks.

It's the same with us. Often, when people feel lonely or sad they automatically reach for something sweet, or alcohol, or even a favourite site on the internet. This gives them a quick lift. Over time it becomes an automatic reaction. To interrupt these pathways, we need to lay down new ones. As a Christian I found this to be an ongoing, lifelong process.

To my delight, as I read the Bible, I found God speaking to me repeatedly.

It was like a word or a sentence jumped off the page and captured my attention. I wrote the different verses in a journal and gradually allowed God's promises to replace my anxious and distrusting mindset. I was aware of my identity changing from being alone and vulnerable to having a deep sense of feeling valued and cared for.

By declaring God's promises out loud, they became familiar to me. I also noticed that they often settled the confusion or sense of anxiety that I had been experiencing. The opposite of anxiety is peace and assurance.

Some of the key verses God used during my early days helped me to see Him as He truly is and not through a strict, religious view of a punitive God. I'd like to share some of these verses, along with what they meant to me at that time.

A Compassionate Father:

"…you are a helper of the fatherless…defending the fatherless and the oppressed." - Psalm 10:14-18 (NIV)

"The Lord is my shepherd, I lack nothing. He makes me lie down in green pastures, he leads me beside quiet waters, he refreshes my soul. He guides

me along the right paths for his name's sake. Even though I walk through the darkest valley, I will fear no evil, for you are with me; your rod and your staff, they comfort me. You prepare a table before me in the presence of my enemies. You anoint my head with oil; my cup overflows. Surely your goodness and love will follow me all the days of my life, and I will dwell in the house of the Lord forever." - Psalm 23 (NIV)

The whole psalm describes the Lord as a gentle, caring Shepherd.

"Though my father and mother forsake me; the Lord will receive me."
 - Psalm 27:10-11(NIV)

"My father and mother abandoned me. I'm like an orphan! But you took me in and made me yours. Now teach me all about your ways and tell me what to do. Make it clear for me to understand, for I am surrounded by waiting enemies." - Psalm 27:10-11(TPT)

I was special to God. I could stop searching because I belonged and I was wanted. God was telling me he would protect and provide for me. He understood how alone I had been. My heart felt full of love for my new Father. I wanted to spend my life pleasing Him.

"A father to the fatherless, a defender of widows…God sets the lonely in families." Psalm 68: 5-6 (NIV)

A Protector:

"Whoever dwells in the shelter of the Most High will rest in the shadow of the Almighty. I will say of the Lord, He is my refuge and my fortress, my God, in whom I trust." Psalm 91:2 (NIV)

"Because He loves me," says the Lord, *"I will rescue him; I will protect him, for he acknowledges my name. He will call on me, and I will answer him; I will be with him in trouble, I will deliver him and honour him. With long life will I satisfy him and show him my salvation."'* - Psalm 91: 14-16 (NIV)
This is a father's protection clearly explained.

"...the lord's unfailing love surrounds the one who trusts in Him."
- Psalm 32:10 (NIV)

A Guide:

"Your word is a lamp for my feet a light on my path."
- Psalm 119:105 (NIV)

I would not be stumbling around in the dark, but would be clearly guided.

"For you created my inmost being; you knit me together in my mother's womb. I praise you because I am fearfully and wonderfully made… all the days ordained for me were written in your book before one of them came to be." - Psalm 139:13- 16 (NIV)

I was someone my Heavenly Father had taken great care in creating. He understood me in a way no one else did. He had written down a plan for my life that He was committed to revealing to me. I encourage you to read the whole psalm; it gave me a brand new identity.

"Trust in the Lord with all your heart and lean not on your own understanding; in all your ways submit to him, and he will make your paths straight. Do not be wise in your own eyes…" - Proverbs 3:5-7 (NIV)

I knew full well how I lacked discernment and was often ambushed by what had been hidden. But now that I had committed my life to God, He promised to guide me. Because He knew best, He would warn me when I was about to make a mistake or was in danger. This gave me great confidence and peace of mind.

I had a heavenly Father who knew best and wanted to communicate with me regularly each day, as I parented my sons and as He unfolded the calling on my life.

A Vindicator:

When Eli was a baby, I needed to attend a court hearing to prove Eli's paternity. This made me feel vulnerable and nervous because I would have to stand in front of professionals. I knew I would feel exposed, embarrassed, and demeaned when they asked me personal questions about my relationship with Eli's father. I had been reading the book of Isaiah just before the hearing date and came across these scriptures.

"Do not be afraid; you will not suffer shame. Do not fear disgrace; you will not be humiliated. You will forget the shame of your youth. And remember no more the reproach of your widowhood. For your Maker is your husband—the Lord Almighty is His name." - Isaiah 54:4-5 (NIV)

These verses expressed what I had been dreading—shame and humiliation—but they were promising me dignity and most amazingly, God's intervention on my behalf. And that is exactly what happened. I was asked some brief questions and then dismissed without feeling at all exposed or humiliated. God had completely fulfilled His promises from Isaiah 54!

"The Lord will call you back as if you were a wife deserted and distressed in spirit—a wife who married young, only to be rejected," says your God."
- Isaiah 54:6 (NIV)

"…with everlasting kindness I will have compassion on you," says the Lord your Redeemer… Though the mountains be shaken and the hills be removed, yet my unfailing love for you will not be shaken nor my covenant of peace be removed," says the Lord, who has compassion on you. Afflicted city, lashed by storms and not comforted, I will build you with stones of turquoise… All your children will be taught by the LORD, and great will be their peace." - Isaiah 54:8-13 (NIV)

This verse impacted me deeply, as I had two children when I read it. God was assuring me that I wasn't alone in the daunting task of bringing them up. Whenever I felt inadequate as a parent and focused on the mistakes I had made, this verse brought me great comfort.

I also declared this verse over my sons regularly for forty years. Declaring God's promises helped me to squash anxiety and to remind myself that God was caring for us all. I have watched His wonderful plan unfolding in my son's lives. Both of them have grown into kind, generous, responsible, God-fearing men. They have both married lovely wives and been blessed with two healthy, intelligent, fun-loving children each. Both my sons have pursued a career in Information Technology and have had unexpected positions and promotions open up to them at key times. I am incredibly grateful to God for His goodness and for fulfilling His promises to us over the past forty years. He is completely trustworthy!

A Sovereign God:

"For I know the plans I have for you,' declares the Lord, 'plans to prosper you and not to harm you, plans to give you hope and a future.'"
- Jeremiah 29:11 (NIV)

There were good things ahead!

"However, as it is written: 'What no eye has seen, what no ear has heard, and what no human mind has conceived – the things God has prepared for those who love him' – these are the things God has revealed to us by his Spirit. The Spirit searches all things, even the deep things of God."
- 1 Corinthians 2:9 (NIV)

This verse thrilled me as it promised something exciting in the future.

"For we are God's handiwork, created in Christ Jesus to do good works, which God prepared in advance for us to do." - Ephesians: 2:10 (NIV)

There was a specific purpose for my life, and God had already organized it!

A Provider:

"This is why I tell you never to be worried about your life, for all that you need will be provided, such as food, water and clothing – everything your body needs." - Matthew 6:25 (TPT)

"So above all, constantly chase after the realm of God's kingdom and the righteousness that proceeds from Him. Then all these less important things will be given to you abundantly. Refuse to worry about tomorrow, but deal with each challenge that comes your way, one day at a time. Tomorrow will take care of itself." - Matthew 6:33 (TPT)

As I embraced the truths of His Word, I learned to see myself through His eyes—as someone of value and with a positive future ahead. All of the painful experiences from my childhood and teens had caused layers of rejection and low self-worth that I had carried with me until the Lord set me free.

My sense of security grew steadily. I now had a kind and compassionate

Father who loved me deeply. He was always watching over me and continually guiding me as I made decisions. Because I learned to trust God, I acted on His nudges in my spirit with boldness and expectation. My confidence grew as I benefited from the positive outcomes of obeying His word. This resulted in the boys and I having a more stable and peaceful life.

The wounds of my painful past were being healed. As I looked at all I had been through, insight and newfound wisdom gave me some tools in my toolbox to help other wounded people I met. I loved bringing comfort and sharing about the power of God's tender love with my neighbours and friends. As a young Christian, I avidly read the Bible. I was amazed at the kindness and protection that God promised to those who trusted in Him. Trust was a major topic in the Bible and an important aspect in a believer's relationship with the Lord.

I was also relieved to discover that He had a plan for my life, as my own plans had ended in pain and failure. I was keen to let someone wiser than me steer the ship! Life throws us into terrifying waves and storms sometimes. They can overwhelm us if we are not anchored to something solid. At times in my life when I have felt overwhelmed, uncertain, or confused, I have used a scripture or a quote to refocus my mind.

Reading through the Bible, I saw that choices made a big difference in people's lives. That was a big, exciting "aha" moment for me, since I had been desperate to understand how to create a stable life for my sons and myself. The answer, in part, was that I needed to make better choices and God was slowly teaching me how to do this.

When I felt inadequate or like a failure, a particular verse in Philippians 1:6 was a great comfort to me: *"…being confident of this, that He who began a good work in you will be faithful to complete it"* (NIV). This encouraged me tremendously, as it reminded me that my loving Father was committed to my growth. Striving and people-pleasing only resulted in suffering burnout until I learned to set healthy limits. God's desire was that I take care of myself and my own needs while serving others.

God's Word was a vital part of my daily life. It is alive and speaks truth, assurance, correction, and guidance to everyone who reads it. Having entered a new Kingdom, I wanted to understand the principles I needed to embrace. My heavenly father made His expectations clear, along with the depth of His commitment to each believer. Life began to make sense to me at last!

God was not some remote, stern, angry god in the sky, waiting to punish us with a big stick if we did something wrong! No. He was a gentle, caring, wise Father who had sacrificed His son so we could have a close, loving relationship with Him and He with each of us. When his children disobeyed Him and hurt themselves, He was waiting with his arms open wide to restore the very one who had rejected him. The story of the Prodigal son illustrates this very clearly (Luke 15:11-32).

At last, I belonged to someone I could trust and with whom I felt safe and cherished. This knowledge changed me enormously over the coming years. Trusting God didn't mean that I didn't experience fear anymore, but rather when fear came I had someone to turn to for help. My confidence was in knowing His character. I knew He was committed to protecting me and this silenced the fear.

Over time, I began to feel confident in my relationship with God and that I was clearly hearing from Him. I felt that my Heavenly Father was delighted when I took risks in my attempts to obey His instructions. I was learning to not overthink things or to play it safe, but to step out boldly into the unknown.

To my great joy, I discovered time and again that He had prepared the way, placing wonderful friends and new opportunities in my path. If I hadn't obeyed, I would have missed out on some great experiences and not understood how powerful and generous He is.

Did I make mistakes? Of course. Making mistakes is a natural part of all learning experiences. I learned this as I watched my toddler struggling to master new skills.

CHAPTER NINE

Blenheim

1983 – APRIL 1985

The same evening that I sensed God speaking to me during worship, directing me to go to Blenheim, I rang Laura McGeorge. She received the news that we were moving to Blenheim calmly, then said that she would ask around to see if there was some suitable accommodation for us. Laura didn't try to discourage me about moving or even question if I had really heard from God. She listened and then agreed to help us. I promptly gave our landlord notice and began to pack up our home. If God said it, then it was a done deal as far as I was concerned.

Meanwhile, Ruth was spending most of her free time with us, which was a great help. She was invaluable, entertaining eight year-old Joshua and caring for Eli. I loved the companionship we had, processing our days and regularly praying together. Ruth was my close buddy, and I realise now that it must have been hard for her, knowing that we were about to move. Ruth had become a valuable family member. She had difficulties with some family dynamics and personal issues connected with this. I was concerned that she would be lonely once we left, but God was working to bring changes in her life too.

A few weeks later, Laura rang me to say that she had found a lovely little cottage that would suit us. It was close to a primary school for Joshua. Her husband Bob and his mate Pete had volunteered to drive down in a truck to collect all our furniture and boxes. I was very grateful and encouraged by their commitment to us. Ruth and I methodically packed everything into large boxes. When we were finished, I said farewell to family and friends, ready to set out on a new chapter in our lives.

I planned to travel up the coast with the boys by train. It would be lovely to just relax and enjoy the stunning scenery after the whirlwind of packing. At the ticket counter, I confidently asked for two seats on the morning train, which was due to leave in thirty minutes. The agent surprised me by stating that all the seats were taken and there was only standing room left. I bought two tickets anyway. God had directed me to move, so I felt assured that He would make a way where there seemed to be none.

I knew I couldn't stand in a swaying carriage for the entire three hours holding a two-year-old, so as I stood on the platform in front of the nearest carriage, I said to God, "Father, according to Isaiah 54, you are my heavenly husband. A good husband would get seats for his wife and the children. I thank you in advance for two seats in this carriage." Having firmly placed the responsibility for seats into God's capable hands, I confidently boarded the carriage. It looked to be full of passengers, but I kept walking down the middle aisle anyway. And then, a miracle happened. At the very end on the last row to the left was an empty double seat. To my great joy, no one was standing nearby. I smiled, said thank you to my precious, faithful Father, and sat down with Eli in my lap. It wasn't long before the train pulled out of the station, chugging along the tracks to our new life. I was elated and quite emotional; once again God had come through for us and fulfilled His promise to take care of all our needs.

When the boys and I arrived in Blenheim, we stayed with Laura and Bob on the farm for two weeks until the little cottage became available. Our cottage was compact and as it was the middle of winter we had a roaring fire going most of the time. The only drawback was that we had an outside toilet. After one particularly cold night, I rushed out to the toilet in the morning, only to discover that I was peeing onto a solid block of ice!

Bob was a shepherd and knew many of the local farmers. One day he took Josh out to see the new lambs at a neighbouring farm, but the next morning an irate farmer rang Bob to tell him that because Josh had cuddled one of the lambs so much, its mother had rejected it. The lamb smelt more like a human (Joshua) instead of her baby and so she refused to feed it. The poor lamb spent the evening bleating until the farmer took it inside to hand feed it with a bottle of warm milk. He already had other lambs that needed looking after and was adamant that Bob come out to fetch the lamb. Bob asked if we wanted it, and of course, the boys said yes! And that's how we ended up with a pet lamb we named Lamb Chops.

She was adorable; soft, white, and fluffy, with a cute little face. Eli and Joshua were both keen to help bottle feed her. They laughed as she tugged at the large teat while wagging her tail with glee. Because it was still cold at nights, I placed her in a cardboard box full of straw in my wardrobe. Our cottage was so small that there was nowhere else to put her! It was funny to wake up each morning and see a small, white lamb's face staring at me from inside my wardrobe. I wondered if Lamb Chops was lonely, so I considered getting a second lamb to keep her company. Josh and I considered names for Lamb Chop's companion. I suggested Mint Sauce as the two names just seem to go together so well.

During the daytime, Eli was at home with me while Joshua was at school. Eli was a self-contained little lad and quite easy to look after. Without friends around me, the first weeks in Blenheim were quite lonely. I didn't know anyone apart from Laura and Bob, so I had a lot of time alone to think, particularly about my relationship with Solomon and the fact that I was raising the boys alone. I still loved Solomon very much and was constantly pleading with God to save him. In my ignorance, I wondered if I wasn't praying enough for him. This led to a lot of uncertainty and confusion around God's role and my role. I gradually became depressed.

One memorable afternoon when Eli was having his nap, I heard the sound of a motor scooter. I had avoided going out for days, as I was feeling so miserable and defeated plus my face was puffy and my eyes were red from all the crying. It would have been embarrassing to let anyone see me in this condition, but now someone was knocking on my door. To my surprise, I saw Pastor Don Judkins from Elim Church standing there. He asked if he could come in. I was hesitant but his caring expression helped me to relax. Don explained that he had been having lunch with his wife when he felt the Holy Spirit prompting him to come and visit me. So he did.

When I explained why I was so upset, he gently said, "Solomon doesn't love you, does he, Chris? If he did, he would be here with you." Gulp! That statement hit me like a ton of bricks. Don had spoken the truth in kindness to help me to stop clinging to a dream and to face the reality of my situation. Over the years, I discovered he was a gentle man with a compassionate heart. Don's statement made me face the fact that Solomon and I were on two different pathways. It was time to let go instead of agonizing over him. My strong desire had been for us all to be one big happy family, but for this to happen, he had to decide to follow Jesus, and that was not happening.

That same week God spoke to me as I was listening to a taped message. The speaker focused on the desires of our heart. He said we can be holding onto something tightly, but God might want us to let it go lest it hurt us. He used the illustration of Moses holding onto the rod. When God said to throw it down, he did and it turned into a snake! I remember this lesson well as I immediately saw how much of my emotional energy and time had been consumed by something I had absolutely no control over. I realised it was important that I let go of the past and focused more on our new life in Blenheim.

Did I grieve, as I released Solomon, along with my deepest hopes for a future together? Yes, absolutely. The letting go process didn't happen overnight; it was a gradual and repeated exercise of giving Solomon back to God. Thankfully, I had gained a healthier perspective about what was best for the boys and me. It sure hadn't done me any good, being consumed by emotions.

One weekend, an Australian evangelist who lived in India came to speak in Blenheim. Laura asked me If I wanted to go with her. She said his messages were often accompanied by demonstrations of God's healing power, so I was keen to attend. I am glad I decided to go as God touched me powerfully during the meeting. Stuart Gramenz told us how he had begun preaching on the streets in India some years before. There he saw many deaf, blind, and crippled people healed by the power of the Holy Spirit. Stuart then founded a ministry called International Outreach and for ten years held enormous crusades where huge numbers of people were saved and healed.

Before we had left Christchurch, a doctor had examined Eli's eyes and told me that he had a lazy eye and would need to wear glasses. The lens on the stronger eye would be covered with a bandage so that the weak eye would work harder to focus. In this way, the weak eye that was turned inwards slightly would gradually grow stronger. I couldn't bear the thought of my gorgeous little son having to wear these glasses, so I had been praying for God to heal him. Stuart began the meeting by telling us about his background and then moved on to describe how people readily received healing in India.

After building up our faith about God's desire to heal us, Stuart asked if anyone needed healing. I told him about Eli's condition and he asked me to come and sit in a chair in front of him with Eli on my lap. After a short prayer, I tried to look at Eli, to see if his eye had been corrected, but he wasn't having a bar of any more attention and buried his face into me! Then I decided that if God wanted to heal us, I would ask Stuart to pray for my sore back, which had been injured when I gave birth to Eli. He instructed me to sit with my back right up against the chair. And as he began to pray I sensed the presence of God immediately. The pain left and I have never had a problem with my back since that time.

I had received a miracle! Furthermore, Eli's eyes have remained strong and healthy, even though his father and some of his siblings all wear glasses. The first time he wore reading glasses was for computer work in his late thirties. God loves to heal us!

Ruth and I had, of course, stayed in touch when I moved to Blenheim. As we talked one day, she surprised me by saying that she had decided to move here also. A job she had lined up fell through and in prayer, she felt God was leading her to move towards independence, while having some close friends and people of faith around her. I was thrilled because I had missed her companionship a great deal. Our little cottage was very small, and naturally Ruth would live with us, so I began looking for something larger and nearer to town and our church. Soon, a lovely two-bedroom flat became available, and we all moved in. The boys shared one room, while Ruth and I shared the second one. Our two single beds and a set of drawers filled up most of the space.

A few months later, a bubbly 17 year-old girl named Debbie came to our church and gave her life to the Lord. She had experienced a lot of difficult situations in her short life, so after discussing Debbie's need for a warm family home, Ruth and I both agreed that we would invite her to live with us. We acquired a bed for her and added it to the two singles already in our room. It was a tight squeeze, creating an even more snug feeling! Debbie was a fun person to have around. She had a wonderful sense of humour and was refreshingly not at all self-conscious about her appearance. She could laugh at herself, as well as others.

Debbie eagerly embraced her newfound faith. She regularly kept us awake because she prayed out loud, enthusiastically communicating with her newfound Saviour without realising she could do this quietly. Debbie never did anything by halves!

After she had been with us for a few months, Debbie decided to move back to her home city of Wellington to look for work. Ruth and I missed her company, but we were glad to have more space in our bedroom. It really had been a very tight squeeze!

Back when we first arrived in Blenheim, Bob and Laura had taken us to their church. Bob was an elder and together they ran a home group one night a week. Elim Church was vibrant with a strong sense of God's presence as we sang songs of adoration to Him. The lead pastor was an excellent Bible teacher who gave many insights into scriptures I had been reading. As Elim also had an excellent Sunday School for Joshua, I decided to make this our home church.

During my first appointment with the senior pastor, Ian Bilby, I shared about the calling on my life to Africa. Then I told him that I was feeling lonely and needed a friend (Ruth had not yet moved up to Blenheim). He replied "You don't need one friend Chris, you need several." He explained that each person played a different role in our lives. One would be a buddy to do things with, another was someone who could listen well and would give good advice, and so on. These words of wisdom proved to be very true. I have repeated them to several people over the years when they too were looking for that one special person to meet so many of their needs.

My first friend was Angie Laird, a young mother of two small children. She and I clicked during our first conversation and began a friendship that we still enjoy today. Angie had a wonderful husband, Gordon, who was kind, gentle, and generous. Together, they have provided much-needed support to the boys and me over the years. One day when I was feeling exhausted Angie came to fetch me and Eli. When we arrived at her home, she gave me a cuppa and then showed me to the spare room where she had a comfy bed all made up with the electric blanket on. Angie told me she would care for Eli while I had a sleep. Her practical kindness was much appreciated, and demonstrated a great sensitivity to my needs.

Each week I attended a Bible study group at the home of Kathy and Gary Fenwick. Gary was a librarian and a knowledgeable man. He was also prophetic. One evening he told us that he had been seeking God, asking for a word for each of us. He said to Lia, a beautiful Dutch lady, that the Lord showed him a picture of a filing cabinet. She was a gifted Bible teacher, and because of her in-depth knowledge of the Word of God, she could teach on many topics. When Gary said this to Lia, I felt quite inadequate. Often when I quoted a verse, I forgot the reference numbers which made me feel embarrassed.

God's personal word for me was also in the form of a picture. It was of a comfy, battered pillow. Gary said I represented someone with whom people felt comfortable. They could rest in my presence. That resonated with me, as people easily opened up—often for the first time in their lives—about the deeper things that had happened to them. Hidden situations that had brought them pain or shame were brought into the light, and healing began. I had been impressed with Lia's word. Compared to a battered old pillow, a filing cabinet full of great teaching sounded a lot more substantial. No wonder we are told not to compare ourselves to others!

The truth was that Lia, while being a skilled Bible teacher, lived with the challenge and disappointment of wanting to teach, but not being allowed to, as only men were accepted as teachers in our church. During this era, men had more authority in the church than women. Consequently, women often had limited opportunities to exercise the wonderful gifts with which God had blessed them. Because of this narrow view, everyone missed out. Thankfully, many doors opened up for Lia in the years ahead. She became the Dean of a Bible college in Papua New Guinea for several years, as well as a New Life minister. Lia has taught in churches all over New Zealand, releasing many believers from the bondage of Freemasonry. It really is true that you can't keep a good woman down.

Elim church had a large modern school, Richmond View which was attached to the church auditorium and office block. The pupils followed a program called Accelerated Christian Education (ACE). Each child was assigned a small cubicle that faced the walls, with partitions either side of them. This system was designed to help pupils focus on their lessons for a set time each day. The goal was for the child to quietly get on with their book work and then put up a little flag to indicate that they had finished. The teacher would then check their work and release them to do a project or group activities.

After several weeks Ros explained to me that Joshua was having difficulty adjusting to the ACE style of learning. Initially he would sing while he focused on his ACE work book, then after a few reminders to be quiet he progressed from singing to humming. Naturally this distracted the other pupils around him.

Richmond View was a private school. It cost more than state run schools but I believed it was a good investment for Joshua's education as the classes were smaller. This meant each child received more attention from the teachers. Ros was a patient person and assured me that Josh would eventually learn to work quietly on his own. The reality was that he was an extrovert who thrived on social interaction, so sitting alone for long periods of time was torture to him.

Years later Josh told me that he found this education system stressful and lonely. I was unaware of this as he hadn't shared how difficult he had found it to adjust.

After three years of what I believed had been a wonderful private education Josh was relieved to say goodbye to cubicles, when we moved away from Blenheim .

One of the highlights for me at that time was that the teachers encouraged families to be involved with many of the interesting activities and projects that were part of the curriculum.
In this way, a strong sense of community was established amongst the teachers, parents, pupils and younger siblings.

Josh tended to drum with anything he had in his hand, including a toothbrush or knives and forks. It frustrated me that he seemed to become so easily distracted when he should be eating his meal or cleaning his teeth. I was constantly admonishing him to sit still or saying "Stop tap, tap, tapping with your cutlery, Josh." Then my mother bought him a small drum kit and I discovered that he was a talented drummer! At last, all that restless energy now had a musical outlet.

Eli, on the other hand, was at the cute toddler stage of learning new skills. When I hung the washing up on the clothesline, he insisted on helping by draping small items over a low wire fence. He was very proud of all his achievements. I enjoyed the company of my contented little boy who had a peaceful, happy nature. Being half African, he had lovely tanned skin and curly dark hair. Often people commented to me that he was such a lovely looking wee lad. Most white people assumed he was part Maori, but Maori people knew straight away that he was not.

One day, when Eli and I were in the doctor's waiting room, a new receptionist asked me where he was from. Realising other patients were listening and waiting for my answer, I became self-conscious, as this was my business and not for public discussion. I looked at the receptionist and replied that he was part African. I expected this to satisfy her, but to my dismay, she then asked me if I had adopted him. With a sinking feeling, I realised where this conversation was going. I quietly replied that I hadn't adopted him. She looked puzzled and then blurted out, "Well, how did you get him?" As I looked behind me, I noticed that the people in the waiting room were all eager to hear the answer to her question. I turned back to the receptionist and boldly said, "Just the usual way." This left her speechless! I quickly sat down and avoided looking at anyone while I waited for the doctor to call my name. Thankfully, few people I encountered took such liberties when seeking answers about my private life!

Eli was blessed, in that he was adored by both Josh and me, as well as Ruth and my friends. At three, he was thankfully a happy, secure little boy with a healthy dose of self-assurance. I realised what an intelligent and observant little lad he was one day after we had been out shopping. I had visited several places with Eli perched on my hip, but when I got to our car, I realised that the keys were missing. I said, "Mummy can't find her keys. She's left them somewhere." I almost fell over when he quietly replied, "They're on the counter at the chemist shop." I was taken aback that he knew exactly which shop they were in. I was also a bit perplexed that he hadn't thought to tell me sooner!

For a short while, I was considering having a relationship with a man I had met at church. He would often visit, sometimes with a gift for me or the boys. Adam was kind, gentle, generous, and easy to be with. Naturally, I enjoyed his attention and being special to someone again. Adam also had a great sense of humour which I enjoyed. One day he arrived at our flat holding a sewing machine. I loved sewing and had missed this creative outlet in my life, so I appreciated having a machine again. After a few months, when I realised I was becoming attached to him, I asked my home group leaders, Gary and Kathy, to invite him over for dinner so they could get to know him. I trusted their judgment about people. Also, others can usually spot when something is not right, whereas, like a friend once said to me, "When you fall in love, your emotions stage a 'coup' in your brain!" Discernment is often overthrown at this time and you only see what you want to see. I needed someone else's input before I decided to invest in this relationship. Having two children to consider made me especially cautious, because they didn't need any more drama in their lives.

After the all-important dinner, Gary rang me to say that Adam had been very open with them. Although he was separated from his wife, he was still legally married to her. This hit me hard, as I knew it would be unwise to continue with our relationship. There was always the possibility that he might get back together with his wife and children at some stage. That night I cried as I went to sleep, and the next morning I rang him to explain that since he was still legally married, I couldn't see him anymore. I asked Adam not to sit next to me in church and to please come and collect all the gifts he had given me and the boys. It was hard returning my treasured sewing machine, but I didn't want any reminders of a relationship that I had decided to end. Once the boys were asleep, I quietly gathered up the toys Adam had brought them and put everything in the garage for him to collect. The next morning everything was gone. After a few weeks, I noticed that Adam was sitting beside another lady each Sunday. He had moved on quickly, but that often happens when someone is lonely.

Shortly after joining Elim Church, I was invited to become part of a wonderful Sunday School team led by Miss Liz Hutton. The passion of her life was training children's workers, and Liz was gifted at this. I became part of a small, tight-knit team which was trained in all aspects of children's ministry: Sunday School work, Bible School classes, holiday clubs, and puppetry. We thoroughly enjoyed being together as a team.

On Sunday mornings, we each took turns to lead worship, present a message, and do skits or puppet shows. It was a wonderful foundation for each one of us, as we practised and grew under the caring eye of Liz Hutton.

One night a week, we took turns to evaluate each other's participation on the previous Sunday. Miss Liz instructed us to make two positive comments to each other before suggesting any improvements as we evaluated each other. In this way, she created a safe and supportive environment for all of us as we learnt. I made wonderful friends during this time who are still my close friends thirty years later. Liz Hutton went on to minister in Papua New Guinea, training children's workers for many years. She left a wonderful legacy for everyone fortunate enough to train and work with her.

The Lord continued speaking to me from His Word and the prophetic words of others about His calling on my life to missions. Often, when a visiting missionary came to church to speak about the work they were doing, they ended their message with an appeal to those who felt God was calling them to minister overseas. I would readily respond, often with a heightened sense of awareness that perhaps this was the person who was going to facilitate a door opening for me. Sometimes I was the only person who responded, so I expected the missionary to be happy that there was someone keen to become a missionary. But usually the response was polite without any real interest in me. On one occasion, the visiting missionary took a step back from me when I began to talk to him about my calling. Because of these encounters, I suffered a fair amount of rejection and sometimes I felt humiliated and dismissed. A regular comment was that I should get involved in children's work. This confused me, as I had been doing just that for several years. After each awkward encounter, I would go back to my seat feeling confused, disappointed and devalued.

Then something special happened. During my time in Christchurch, I had met Dave and Vicky Beaumont, who were missionaries in Zimbabwe. They were encouraging to me and suggested I contact a lady called Katie who ran a children's ministry in Zimbabwe. They wondered if I might even join her in the future, as I was an experienced children's worker. Then to everyone's surprise, not long after independence, the new government of Zimbabwe refused visas for several missionaries including the Beaumonts and Katie. They returned to New Zealand for awhile before heading out to different nations.

During one school holiday, Liz arranged for our team of children workers to attend a training camp at a beautiful beach site. When I arrived, I met a lovely young lady called Katie from Zimbabwe! I was so amazed, that of all the people who could have come to help train us, Liz had chosen someone with whom I had been hoping to connect. This incident encouraged me tremendously. I had several days in which to get to know Katie and to discover more about Zimbabwe. This precious time together felt like a very timely, special gift to me from my Father, who knew the deepest desires of my heart. Experiences like this encouraged me to keep praying for and pursuing the missionary call to Africa.

During this time, I also began a two-year diploma course called Church and Family. It was quite in-depth and required homework each week. Our senior pastor, Ian Bilby, presented the course one night a week. We were trained to research and present a message on either a biblical character or a specific theme to the group. As I love learning, I thrived in this small class environment, thoroughly enjoying the company of others who were also hungry to grow in their Christian walk.

However, by the second year my life had become increasingly busy because as well as raising the boys, I was also involved in many other activities. These included being out four nights a week at church meetings such as home group, children's church leader's meetings, and the Church and Family training sessions. Each Sunday morning I participated in children's church, then attended a service in the evening. It all became too much for me. After two years of constant activity I was close to exhaustion and was no longer enjoying life. After much wrestling in my mind, I decided that I needed to speak to one of the four pastors on staff to explain that all the activity and responsibilities had become too much for me.

This was a difficult thing to do, because, much of what we did as

Christians in those days was performance-based. As believers, many of us had the idea that busyness was equal to commitment to God. Of course, this was not true, but we were given subtle messages to attend everything and to give generously when asked. Some of my friends simply stopped attending church when the pressure and workload became too much for them, especially when their family life suffered. They still loved the Lord, but were happier escaping from the constant activity, and instead chose to worship together with a few friends.

I had been given an appointment with Pastor Doug, as Pastor Bilby was away. Feeling quite nervous and inadequate, I hesitantly explained all the different activities I was involved with every week and expressed my desire to take a short break from the course that I had been doing for the past eighteen months. As I had nervously walked to his house that morning I had been hoping and praying that he would be kind and understanding. Instead, with a stern expression, he quoted a verse from Luke 9:62, which stated that "No one who puts a hand to the plough and looks back is fit for service in the kingdom of God." He told me that I was to finish what I had started.

Feeling like a naughty schoolchild who's been caught trying to wangle their way out of something that they should be doing, I slunk out of his house. His wife showed me to the door without a smile or even a kind word. Along with all the pressure of feeling exhausted—overwhelmed by life's demands and the church leaders expectations—I now felt like a wayward, irresponsible shirker. Needless to say, I no longer enjoyed attending church services, as once again I felt judged and defective as a person. Feeling dejected and trapped, I walked back to an empty house. Ruth had recently gone flatting with a friend, so there was no one with whom to share my horrible experience. A good cry and some encouraging words were definitely what I needed at this point but instead I felt judged, misunderstood, and very alone.

Then God opened a wonderful door for the boys and me. Liz asked me if we would like to share a large furnished house with her. Liz was a gentle and kind person with a natural servant's heart, so the time with her became like a balm to my bruised soul. Most importantly though, the boys loved being with her.

Two significant things happened for us during the year we lived with Miss Liz.

The first was that my mother came to stay with us for a holiday, which turned out to be a wonderful time of bonding and enjoying each other's company. Mum became quite the happy extrovert when she was on holiday and the boys adored being with their precious Nana. Mum enjoyed the beautiful scenery around Blenheim as well as attending Sunday worship at our vibrant church.

The second event was that Josh's dad (who rang him occasionally) invited him to visit Sydney for a holiday with him and his new family. Joshua was nine years old by now and ecstatic that he was about to see his dad again. The thought of flying by himself to another country was very exciting.

Soon after Joshua left, Eli, three, had been asking me to do something for him and I was hesitating. After the third request, when I replied that I would think about it, his eyes lit up and he said, "Josh told me that when you say you will think about it, I need to keep asking because you will give in." I was speechless as I contemplated the fact that, not only had Josh sussed me out so well, but he had coached his little brother in the art of pressuring and manipulating Mum! Needless to say, I changed the way I responded to the lads' requests from then on.

When Josh came back home, he was excited about all he had seen and done. His father had been surprised at how independent Josh was. He would bus into the city with his father each morning, then set off alone to explore all the sights and shopping malls before meeting up with Mike again at the end of the workday.

Spending weeks with his father had been wonderful for Josh. Little Eli was listening wistfully to all this and asked me if he could also speak to his dad. By now, I had lost contact with Solomon; once he had completed his degree, he had settled back into Zimbabwe. I knew it was important for Eli to connect with Solomon, so I made enquiries with his family, who still corresponded with me. After a few attempts, I managed to locate him at his workplace. Josh and I stood close by as Eli spoke into the phone, greeting his father. It was very touching, watching as he spoke with his dad. Eli's little eyes lit up and a big smile spread across his face. I was happy for him and also glad that I hadn't spoken negatively about their fathers to either of my sons. I felt it was important that Josh and Eli got to know their fathers and formed their own opinions about them. It would have been sad if their relationships had been damaged because of my experiences. I had seen too many children hurt and confused when one parent ran another one down. As a consequence, the children often missed out on an important part of their lives.

After seeing how being connected to their fathers for even a short while had positively impacted the boys, I became concerned that they were growing up without a male role model in their daily lives.

My sister Sophie, who had been instrumental in my coming to the Lord in Christchurch, had moved to a small town called Coniston in the North Island. This town was close to where her husband Trev had grown up. He worked at the huge pulp and paper mill on the outskirts of Coniston. In summer there was always a pervasive smell of wood shavings in the air. Sophie and I talked regularly on the phone. On one occasion I mentioned to her that I was concerned about the lack of male role models in the boys' lives and without hesitation, she invited me to move up and to stay with them until we found our own place.

I felt like my time in Blenheim had ended, so once again I farewelled my friends and headed up north to join Sophie and her family. Our little car was full, with many treasured items packed into every available space.

Looking Back

In an interesting twist to this story, I heard that Pastor Doug resigned about a year after I left. Recently I met him at a social gathering where we spent time chatting about our journeys. Doug was open and honest, sharing about how the Lord had led him to a very fulfilling ministry, which he enjoyed very much. I could see he was now a relaxed person. I was glad that we had the opportunity to meet again as two fellow travellers who both loved the Lord very much. Thank goodness I had forgiven him and had not burdened myself with bitterness and a hardened heart for hurting me so long ago. The two senior pastors also moved on; one worked in the secular arena for a time and the other was employed by a Christian organisation.

I learned over time that God is more interested in establishing a heart to heart relationship with everyone. I spent years volunteering for many things in the hope of being approved of and accepted. Unfortunately, this only led to disappointment and burnout. God desires for each of us to grow in our faith, getting to know His word, His character, and His ways. In a close, loving relationship where we feel safe enough to be open and real, there is no need to hide our mistakes or failings. Our Heavenly Father does not condemn, criticise, or push us away.

As I write, it's August 2020, and just this morning I read some powerful scriptures out of the 'Passion' translation from Psalm 119:35b-36:

"I will set my heart before you to understand your ways. I have learned that there is nothing perfect in this imperfect world except your words, For they bring such fantastic freedom into my life!"

It truly is liberating to forgive. As the Word states, *"There is nothing perfect in this imperfect world,"* which means that we will get many opportunities in our lifetime to forgive others as well as ourselves!

Bob and Laura McGeorge - wonderful friends

CHAPTER TEN

Coniston

1985

After a tiring two day drive from Blenheim, it was an enormous relief to arrive at Sophie and Trev's home. Sophie was a warm, generous, and funny person. She always made time to listen to people's problems and comfort them, usually with a cup of tea and some freshly baked cake. Trev was a laid back, family-oriented man who also had a great sense of humour. I was looking forward to a relaxing week with them both after the demands of moving and driving upcountry.

However, the day after I arrived Sophie informed me that she had decided to give up smoking. Her plan was to seclude herself in her bedroom while she went through withdrawal, leaving me to run their home. I was happy to support her by cooking, cleaning, and making sure all four boys (my two and their two) got to school on time. After a few days, when the worst of the craving had left, Sophie ended her self-imposed seclusion. She had conquered her smoking habit, which was no small achievement. I was proud of her.

Eli thoroughly enjoyed being with his cousins, one of whom was his age. Josh was the eldest of the four and was happy to be near his Aunty Sophie again. We had all spent a lot of time together back in Christchurch before they moved up north. Philip Junior and Eli both began primary school around the same time. After his first day at school, Eli disappeared. When I went to find him, he was curled up on his bunk bed under the blankets, complete with his school bag on his back! I realised something was amiss and asked him what the matter was. To my surprise, he announced that he wasn't going back to school again because he didn't know how to read! I chuckled to myself before coaxing him into the kitchen for some afternoon tea.

Josh, who was 11 at the time, attended the local intermediate school. He had already attended several different schools and was not enjoying the experience of starting over again. He was an outgoing and sociable person so he soon made friends, but because he was well-mannered and different, he was bullied by a group of rough boys. They considered him to be an outsider, someone easy to pick on. I was not aware of this until he became stressed and reluctant to attend school. After he opened up to me, we talked about the situation. I was prepared to speak with the headmaster but Josh wanted to handle it by himself. He gradually made his own set of friends and confronted one of the bullies in a fist fight, which he won. After that, the bullying eased.

With four adults and four children all living together in a three bedroom home, a desire to live in my own place grew. Just as I was considering looking for somewhere to rent, my Mum came to visit and gave Sophie and me an unexpected financial gift. This enabled us both to put a deposit on a modest home. It was an exciting time for us as we looked at different homes on sale and then chose one each. I was keen to redecorate and create some beautiful gardens in the bare patches outside my new home. How wonderful, to each be the proud owner of a lovely three-bedroom home.

At this time, I decided to give up focusing on my missions call to Africa. After all the frustrations and misunderstanding of the past, I just wanted an ordinary life with my sons. It had been several years since God had shown me the vision of the waterfall and no opportunity for overseas mission work had opened up. For all I knew, I might only go when I was in my fifties or sixties, so I concentrated on my sons and enjoyed making plans to redecorate our new home. There was no longer any excitement when God stirred my spirit about this calling. The reality was that it had been a source of confusion for five long years, so I pushed it to one side and settled down to being a regular mum.

During the week I taught a few Bible in School classes at the local primary schools. Many nights I sat up until after midnight, creating lovely flannel backgrounds with new scenes for each story I told. One hot afternoon while I was gardening at home, I heard one of the young lads from school calling out to me from our gate. He and a friend showed me a newly hatched baby bird that they had found lying on the ground. The poor little mite didn't have a single feather on its entire body. The boys said to me "Miss, you have been teaching us that God answers prayer and we want you to keep this baby bird and pray for it to stay alive." I looked at the pitiful scrap lying in their hands and was not sure he would even last a few hours. The boys handed him over with trusting looks and happily went off home. I had a big challenge on my hands now and put "Harry" into a shoe box filled with grass, praying he would survive. The shoe box sat on the kitchen counter top where I could feed him every four hours with tiny bits of bread dipped in milk.

To my delight, each morning Harry was in his shoe box chirping away, waiting for his breakfast. He even accompanied me to the classes, perched in my pocket, where he began to chirp as the children sang. The kids loved it when I showed them that Harry was growing new feathers. He came to school for several weeks, until one morning when I went to feed him and discovered that he had died in the night! I was not looking forward to telling the children, but I wove it into a story about the cycle of life and death!

My love of adventure almost ended in disaster one memorable day when I met a pilot at the local shops. Ben told me that he owned a small plane and was flying it across the country the next morning to attend

*Above: With my mentor and
great friend, Bev Robertson*

*Right:
Me, about 1986*

a plane exhibition. My immediate reaction was, "Wow, that sounds like a fun experience." Because I had never flown in a small plane I asked if I could come too, along with Eli and his friend Archie. Ben agreed and so we all set off the next morning with high expectations for this exciting trip in his Cessna 721.

The reality was that we were squashed into a tiny, noisy plane. As we steadily droned across the country for a couple of hours, the adventure had become an endurance test. Eli looked miserable and then threw up into a plastic bag which I had to throw out of the small passenger window.

Once we landed, we were all feeling slightly dazed and wishing we had stayed home! The boys and I were dreading the return trip later that afternoon. We spent some time looking at the aircraft displays before boarding the Cessna. Halfway home we encountered a violent rainstorm. Ben announced he needed to take a detour along the coast where it would be safer to fly. While bouncing around high up amongst the black clouds I decided that this would definitely be our last trip in a small plane!

Eventually our skilled pilot landed us all safely and three very jaded, pale-faced passengers rapidly descended to the familiarity of firm ground. There was not much conversation on the walk home as we were all quite shaken from the storm. The sense of being in danger had been very real. Once home, a muffled statement of "You and your adventures" was flung in my direction. I couldn't respond, as I too was in shock at the exciting "adventure" that had delivered far more than we could have possibly imagined.

Soon after arriving in Coniston we began to attend Sophie and Trev's church. I enrolled in a Bible study group taught by the senior pastor. He was an excellent teacher as well as having a great sense of humour. Every Friday night, a programme called Royal Rangers was held for children of all ages. It was similar to Scouts, with badges being awarded to those who mastered certain skills. The group I led was for five-year-olds and was called Straight Arrows. As Sophie, Trev, and I were all leaders, we had great family times with the boys, camping at nearby lakes while they practised their outdoor skills.

The church leadership had some strict rules. One was that a man did not enter a home if only a lady was present. The intention was to guard against immorality. However, as a single mum, I discovered that this same rule, when taken to extremes, had some drawbacks like the occasion when we were walking to church in the rain and a fellow church member drove past us without offering us a lift. I felt disappointed that protocol had prevented him from applying common sense and giving us a lift.

Each year a large mission's conference was held in a neighbouring town.

The assistant pastor's wife, Denise, invited me to attend the conference with her. I was eager to go because the guest speaker, David Wang, was someone I had read about in the Asian Outreach magazines. Josh also came and then disappeared. As the worship began, I was looking around for him. Suddenly, my friend next to me jabbed me in the ribs and said, "Look at the musicians, Chris." To my amazement, I saw Josh on the stage confidently playing the drums! One of the other musicians was nodding his head to give Josh the beat at the start of each song. After worship, Josh joined us, looking very pleased with himself and enjoying the expression of almost disbelief on my face.

Later the leader of the worship team told me that Josh had a natural talent and would make a fine musician. He asked if he could train him for an outreach team that travelled and ministered in prisons. This seemed like a great opportunity for Josh to be with godly men, so even though he was only twelve, I agreed. On Friday nights, the outreach team would come by to collect Josh for the weekend. When he arrived home I enjoyed listening as he shared about his experiences.

Growing up in a home where we were not free to address painful situations, I developed a habit of speaking out when I saw children being mistreated. It is often easier to just ignore or to stand on the sidelines, but I got involved if I saw someone suffering. One morning in the 1980s when I was out shopping, I passed by a man and woman who were arguing very loudly while their distressed little boy stood helplessly by, watching them. I took the boy by the hand and said to the parents, "You are scaring your son, so I am taking him to a nearby café for a soft drink. When you have finished arguing, you can come and get him." Holding the little lad's hand, we walked to a nearby café and waited for them to collect him, which they did eventually.

Another time, I saw an angry woman pushing an adult-sized bicycle into the back of a crying little girl while she shouted at her. I stopped, greeted the lady, and asked her what the problem was. I was curious to know what had made the mother so upset that she was deliberately hurting her child. The mother told me that her daughter had lost her new shoes and there was no more money to replace them. Being a single mother on a limited income myself, I understood how frustrated she was, so I calmed her down and then took them both to a nearby shoe shop to buy replacement shoes. Both these situations were ones that I could not ignore. I didn't realise it at the time, but these incidents were setting the scene for what I would be called on to do in the future: be a voice for those who had none.

My older sister, Margy, lived in the large city of Auckland, a few hours away from Coniston. She often invited the boys and I up to have wonderful holidays with her and her family. Margy was married to Fred, an entrepreneur who began several, successful food businesses. The kids loved visiting his takeaway or restaurants whenever we stayed with them. The huge smoked ham we came home with each year was a great hit also! The year I turned thirty-five, Margy, who had just had major surgery, rang me to ask if I would come up for several weeks to care for her and run her home. This time together turned out to be pivotal for us both as we spent many afternoons speaking openly about our experiences as children for the first time in our lives. Margy had been our Dad's favourite child, which was hurtful and often made me angry. I was sarcastic to her, which naturally prevented us from becoming close. Margy surprised me by sharing how lonely she had been at home, often wishing we were friends. It was wonderful to be able to talk so freely to each other and to forge a strong sisterly bond for the first time.

After doing the housework and running some errands, I would join Margy on her large water bed, while we ate treats and watched her favourite programme called 'The Oprah Show.' The host was an American lady called Oprah Winfrey. Margy and I enjoyed listening as she interviewed different people who were often struggling with their marriage or had family problems. This was my first experience of hearing people publicly sharing about their difficult situations. We were amazed at this straight-talking lady who addressed uncomfortable topics, answering with wisdom and compassion. So many participants spoke of having been betrayed or abused. I was riveted, learning that it is important to speak about what happens to us. I had been silenced for much of my childhood.

Another TV show host I learnt from was Dr. Phil. Speaking on the issue of trust, he said, *"You don't trust or distrust people when you first meet them. What you need to do is observe their behaviour until you know if they are trustworthy people or not."* Listening to programmes like these, I realised that my family had lived in a world where we hid the truth about what was happening at home. Keeping the peace and not rocking the boat were important goals. Very little was addressed or discussed at home, so there was little improvement, healing, accountability, or closure. I grew up with a deep sense of injustice and frustration at serious situations being swept under the carpet. As an adult, I realised that in many homes, avoidance, denial, and excuse-making was the way people handled unpleasant situations in my grandparents' and parents' generations.

As I gained insights from these relationship "gurus," I was able to recognise many factors that had contributed to the dysfunctional dynamics of our home life. I also recognised what had happened in my broken marriage. Soaking up all these life skills gave me insight and clarity. I felt empowered because I now had a new standard and some tools I could use in difficult situations. As a young solo mum with two little boys, I was deeply concerned that the boys lacked a positive male role model during their formative years. While reading books about bringing up children, I discovered some disturbing statistics concerning the percentage of men in prison who came from a single-parent home. I now realise that this made me anxious about the boy's future because they fitted into the high-risk category. The result was that I became hyper-vigilant with them and especially watchful of the friends they made. My secret fears caused me to become too strict and controlling of the boys at times. As I have gained insight into my past behaviour I have apologised to them both. At that time, James Dobson's books were a huge blessing to me in learning how to raise the boys. They gave clear guidance and provided me with structure. Growing up in my own family, I hadn't seen healthy, well-defined roles where we all felt accepted and safe.

This was what I wanted for my sons, so I purchased and read material on different topics, such as raising children to take responsibility, helping children to develop self- control, the art of discipline, establishing traditions, and much more. I was like a thirsty sponge, desiring to acquire as much knowledge as possible. When I noticed a family that looked strong and happy, I would spend time with the mother and ask her for keys to her approach. I did this for many years, making wonderful friends along the way, and gradually developing my style. As I developed structure in our home, I grew in confidence as a mother, having learned skills from wise, knowledgeable, godly mentors. It was very empowering to have a map for the way forward instead of letting my emotions dictate my decisions. Josh was six when I became a Christian, so he had a rocky start, with a confused and emotional Mum in his early years. Eli was born after I had surrendered my life to God when I was basing decisions on God's Word as well as the advice of mature Christians.

The years we spent in Coniston were wonderful as well as challenging. Focusing on our family, camping with my sister and her family, and enjoying the beautiful outdoors around us provided some wonderful memories. Josh was a wonderful big brother to Eli, entertaining him for hours and introducing him to LEGO and then to computers as they got older. Eli was a calm, content little boy who grew up surrounded by people who adored him.

During our six years in Coniston, I raised my sons alone, maintained our home and gardens, worked hard at different time jobs, and was involved in children's ministry throughout. This was good grounding for the years ahead where I would be regularly involved in team work and landscaping and renovating old buildings. My ten years of preparing messages for Bible in Schools laid a solid foundation for future ministry. Even when I didn't think some aspects of my life in Coniston were of much significance, I would later see how God had been busy developing my faith, trust, and ability to handle responsibilities with grit and determination. Nothing is wasted in God's wise hands.

CHAPTER ELEVEN

Lord Give Me Strength

1986 - 1987

A solo parent's role is relentless. Every decision that needs to be made stops with you. I could usually cope, but living in a small town on a tight budget, I began to feel quite run down. When I talked with my doctor, he asked me several questions, then told me I had all the classic symptoms of depression. He offered to prescribe Valium for me, but I refused. I was horrified at being depressed, feeling that I had somehow let God down; I had bought into the lie that Christians should always be happy and strong. I cried as I walked home, trying to process how I had gotten into this condition. The answer was obvious of course. I was raising two growing lads on my own. With a limited budget and all the responsibility, I regularly became exhausted and without a vehicle, there were few outings or fun days away from our small town.

By the time I reached home, I had created a strategy for myself. I realised that due to the depression, I had been spending time in bed during the day. To stop this new habit, I decided I would close my bedroom door after making my bed each morning and not go back until the evening. Each morning after breakfast I headed outside to the large flower and vegetable gardens that I had created. Gardening was therapeutic and something I had always loved doing. Another option was to go to the heated swimming pool in the town centre. It was within walking distance and best of all, access was free because the water was heated from underground thermal springs. Since I was not a strong swimmer, I watched other people and copied their movements. In this way, I learnt a new skill and found somewhere relaxing to spend time. Lying on my back in the water, looking up at the brilliant blue sky, I became aware of how relaxed I felt. I was doing something enjoyable away from all my responsibilities and as a result, my soul was soothed and I felt free.

A few days after seeing the doctor, I heard a man speaking on the radio about what elderly people wished they had done differently throughout their lives. After participating in a survey on their top regrets in life, two main themes were highlighted. Many wished they had taken more risks and also that they hadn't worried so much. The facilitator of the programme said that 90% of our fears never come to pass. I was astonished at that fact, because I frequently caught myself worrying about the future. I realised that I needed to nip that futile habit in the bud!

An article I read stated that when we are relying solely on ourselves, we can become anxious because we are finite beings and have limited knowledge, resources, and strength. The key to peace was to abandon our trust in ourselves and turn our life over to our powerful, loving, and resourceful Heavenly Father. Then we don't need to know what is up ahead for us; we can rest in His character and integrity "for He who promises is faithful" (Heb. 10:23, NIV). God's Word assures us that His plans are good for us, to give us "a future and hope" (Jer. 29:11, NIV). Because of His commitment to us, we can feel peace, even in the middle of negative situations and uncertainty. I knew I had been worrying about several things I had no control over: lack of money, the boys growing up without a dad, and the elusive missions calling to Africa.

Soon after this an interesting and unexpected door opened up for me, which provided us with more income. The local schools were struggling to find trained relief teachers to fill in when regular teachers were on leave or sick. One teacher, who was also part of our Royal Rangers team, asked me to consider becoming a relief teacher. She knew I had never been trained, but saw that I enjoyed working with children and handled challenging children well. Because it was a paid role, close to home, and a fresh challenge, I accepted her invitation and thus began a new career at the local primary schools and the secondary school. It was a daunting role initially and I felt out of my depth amongst all the professional teaching staff, but they were friendly and supportive, knowing I would be challenged repeatedly in most of the classes I took.

For three years, I received phone calls most mornings asking me to fill in for a teacher who was sick or away on a field trip. The teacher would leave written instructions for the subject I was to teach, which I tried to implement despite some older pupils who thought they could intimidate or distract me. They didn't realise that I had been dealing with strong, vocal boys for years.

My first experience of taking a new entrants class (five-year-olds) was a real eye-opener, as I had assumed they would be a demure little bunch. However, I soon discovered how wrong my expectation was because they were the trickiest students of any age group. These little ones had bonded strongly with their teacher and expected me to closely follow her daily routine. I read her notes and then began to write the date on the blackboard. As I progressed to the letter for the day, I heard shrieks of laughter and several loud voices calling out, "You've done it wrong Miss, the 'g' is not supposed to have a curly tail." It was not pleasant having thirty small children all staring at me, while they loudly voiced their disapproval. A quick swipe with the duster removed the offending tail after which the children settled down and much to my relief began writing rows of g's in their books (without the curly tail of course).

I felt quite embarrassed after their outburst, but the worse was to come later that day when I realised some pupils were missing from the class. Upon inquiring if anyone knew where Hinemoa and Wiremu were, I was informed with great enthusiasm that they were in the toilet having a water fight! Oh no! I raced off to find a small band of five-year-olds enjoying water play. By lunchtime, I was exhausted. One child had bitten another and I had spent valuable class time sorting this out. That evening I decided that the next time I was asked to take the new entrants class, I would have a large bag of sweets with me to bribe them into submission all day!

At the secondary school I faced entirely different challenges with the teenagers. Among the focused students were some who had fathers in the local gangs. Others were from broken homes, where there was little authority or guidance. Their natural reaction to being given instructions was to challenge the relief teacher. As some of the lads were big in stature, they could appear quite intimidating when they were determined to oppose me. The rest of the class would carefully watch how I handled the situation hoping, no doubt, that I would capitulate and leave them to do their own thing for the hour. Even though it was daunting managing classes of older students who enjoyed making things difficult for me, I enjoyed the challenge of getting them settled.

The most difficult confrontation I experienced was with a sixteen-year-old who was the class tough guy. Dave refused to sit at his desk and begin the maths classwork. I wrote him out a detention note and handed it to him while the class watched the unfolding drama. To my surprise he simply scrunched the detention paper up and threw it into

Left: In my Salvation Army uniform with Josh and Eli

Right: Eli with his best buddy

my face, declaring that I couldn't make him work. The room was silent. The students had not begun work either, hoping I would simply quit and leave them be. I knew if I did not handle Dave's outburst well I wouldn't be respected in any of the classes in the future. So I ignored him and very firmly repeated my instructions to the students. As they began to open their books and start on the maths assignment, I quietly slipped out of the classroom and headed straight for the headmistress's office. After explaining what had just taken place, she asked me to send Dave to her. I calmly re-entered the classroom and gave him the message, which wiped the smirk off his face. Dave was suspended that day for two weeks, which had the effect of the older students not challenging me as much. There was no illusion left of me being an easy target or a softie. Little did they know that I had been shaking inside when he challenged me and also that I cried as I biked home complaining to God that there must be easier ways to earn a living. The next time I was assigned to that same class, I was greeted by a lad who said, "You're the teacher who got Dave suspended." I calmly replied, "No, he did that to himself."

Despite the odd tough student, I enjoyed my time at the college, although I was a mystery to the pupils. One day I would be covering an art class and the next maths, typing, or home economics. Over time the students became curious because of the wide variety of subjects I covered. One bold lad asked me what were the actual subjects that I was qualified to teach. Of course, I couldn't let on that I had never trained even in one subject as a teacher, so I answered with a vague "Wouldn't you like to know!"

Maths was one of the more difficult classes, because the curriculum had changed so much since I was at school. This created a problem for me, but as I prayed I began to see a way out. My strategy was to hold the opened exercise book the students were working from in my hands and then on top of it, where they couldn't see, I had the teacher's answer book.

I asked the students to raise their hand when they had completed a particularly tricky equation, which was beyond my understanding. One of them was chosen to write it out on the blackboard at the front of the class, so everyone, including me, learnt how it was done. In this way, I "taught" maths and other subjects to each unsuspecting class. I became good at bluffing my way through many classes while looking authoritative and competent. If only they had realised how inadequate I often felt.

Interestingly enough, the principal told me on my last day of teaching that she regularly gave me the toughest classes because she knew I could handle them! Little did she know how much I prayed for wisdom, as well as sometimes crying with exhaustion at home. In a lovely gesture of thanks, she came by one day and presented me with a beautifully embroidered bedspread. This made me feel very special and appreciated. Years later I realised that teaching at the college had helped me to become a stronger and more decisive person. It had been a handpicked training ground to prepare me for similar settings in the future.

During our time in Coniston, I was fortunate to have a wonderfully kind and wise mentor, Bev Robertson. She and her husband Ian were lay preachers at the local Anglican church. Bev was also a board member of Women's Aglow (now known as Aglow International), which was at its peak during this time. She counselled me whenever I wasn't coping or was facing a difficult situation. When I was diagnosed with depression, Bev took me on outings out of town. One memorable afternoon we drove to the local hot pools where we swam and ate fresh strawberries while we sat on the grass chatting. Bev showed her concern in practical ways, which I valued and appreciated. She was the opposite of me in some ways. I had moved constantly from the age of sixteen while she had only ever lived in two homes during her life. I enjoyed watching Bev and Ian laughing at each other's foibles and having robust discussions on different topics. Observing their healthy marriage made me realise what was possible for a family. The distrust I had previously lived with was gradually healed and replaced with a more positive image of marriage.

Twice a year, Mum and my stepfather John came to Coniston for a few weeks holiday. They stayed in a caravan at Sophie's place.

During our last few months in New Zealand, Mum came over to spend a night with the boys and me.

I put fresh linen on her bed and the boys filled a small basket with goodies to let her know how much she meant to us. After dinner we had an enjoyable evening, playing board games and catching up. The boys had lots to tell her about their hobbies and school friends.

It was a special time for us all as Mum knew we were selling the house and heading off to Africa. I was very aware that it might be several years before we saw her again. My Mum has always been a caring and generous person who loves to give whenever she sees a need.

I appreciated her financial support and the thoughtful gifts because being a single parent meant that my finances were often limited. On one occasion Mum arrived at our home with a lovely keyboard she had just bought for me. She knew I longed to learn to play the piano. On other occasions when the boys were needing new clothes or a bill needed to be paid, money would arrive in the mail wrapped in foil and tucked into a letter. Mum's legacy to my siblings and myself has been to instill compassion in us for people in need. My sisters and I have had combined careers of working with deaf children, special needs adults, the elderly, widows and orphans. Mum, Margy and Sophie all trained and worked in the nursing field for many years.

During school holidays, I volunteered as a camp 'Aunty' at Raglan Holiday camps. These camps were run by a Christian organization near a beautiful beach. Many children's workers from around the country came to serve a large number of energetic, excited children. For two weeks, they enjoyed stories, singing, outdoor walks, and time with new friends. I slept in a bunk bed in a room with eight young boys. One boy called Nigel, was a particular favourite of mine. He was a big lad with learning difficulties who also had a challenging home life. Nigel loved food, especially spaghetti. As he was very affectionate, I often ended up with spaghetti in my hair or on my clothes when he enthusiastically plonked himself in my lap for a cuddle. He insisted that I slept next to his bunk so he could touch my face as he went to sleep. As his hygiene wasn't too brilliant, I was privy to the interesting smells emanating from his bunk.

During the second year at camp, I realised that Alan, the main male teacher and counsellor, was taking a particular interest in me. I was flattered as he had been in ministry for twenty years and was like a son to the leaders. He also worked at a Salvation Army children's home and was raising two foster sons. As I spent time with him, he appeared to be a wonderful, sacrificial, and dedicated person. Alan was known for being sensitive to children's needs, spending hours counselling them.

I was delighted in February 1987 when Alan proposed to me and presented me with a stunning diamond and sapphire engagement ring.

My heart was so thrilled that the boys would have such a wonderful man for a father figure. It seemed that all my years of praying for this had been answered. The leaders and staff put on a lovely engagement party where I met some of Alan's friends who had known him for many years. He seemed to be well respected by everyone. Then something strange happened. That night as I stood by the huge windows overlooking the sea, I had a strong sense that I was going to be very lonely in my marriage to Alan. He was a friendly, kind man, but the feeling stayed with me during the next day. Then when he was with me, I noticed that he said all the right things—calling me darling and telling me that he loved me—but his eyes looked blank. It was as if he was detached from his emotions. This unsettled me a great deal. I mustered my courage and decided to speak to the leaders about my concerns; he was like their son, whereas they had only known me for two years.

To their credit, when I said that I felt there was something wrong, they agreed. They had also noticed that something was not quite right and promised to speak to him about this. Camp ended the next day, which left me in a state of nervousness as I drove back home with my two sons. Alan's twin foster sons joined us because they had wanted to spend time with their soon-to-be mum and brothers. During the following days, I was surprised at their emotional state and some strange behaviour they exhibited. The older one would sit on the garage roof or behind the couch, refusing to join us for meals, while the younger one told me the things he wanted to be put in his coffin when he died.

Their behaviour disturbed me, especially as they had been living with someone who was a wise, caring counsellor. It didn't seem to add up.

Then, I received a letter from Alan in the post. I had been wondering how he would react after I had asked his leaders to speak with him. The answer was in the letter! He reacted swiftly and harshly by calling off the engagement. Alan even blamed me for agreeing to marry him. He felt I had been too quick to accept his proposal! I was so horrified at what I was reading that I let out a scream, then I rushed next door to show my friend Sally. As she read the letter, I became calm and matter of fact, accepting the fact that there was to be no marriage and no father for the boys. The calm was soon replaced with anger at him for messing me around and disappointing us all.

The next day I took the letter to Pastor Tom and Pam to ask for their advice. Even though Tom was quite strict on some issues, he had a fatherly heart. During one visit, when he and Pam visited my home, he slipped out after peaking in my cupboard and arrived back with a huge box of groceries! He had sensed I was struggling and without any comment, he acted in the best way possible. Tom told me that he would contact Alan to ask him what was happening. After the call, Tom said to wait two months while Alan sought direction from God. At this stage, I was over the idea of a relationship and just wanted to bring closure. I knew after receiving such a horrible letter from Alan that I could never trust him again. I wanted to go straight down and give him the ring back, but within days something enormous and traumatic happened that prevented me from doing this.

On the second of March, at lunchtime, the first of two major earthquakes struck our region. The first one measured magnitude 5.2, followed by a mag. 6.3 earthquake. They were situated close by and because they were quite shallow, they caused major damage to houses, roads, and railway lines. I was on the phone to my sister Sophie when I noticed the power lines swaying and the windows buckling in and out. I shouted "Psalm 91" to her as she rushed off to get her baby. The sound around me was terrifying. Everything began falling out of cupboards and off the shelves. The violent force of the main tremors sent my vast array of preserves (that I had spent weeks bottling), toppling out of the cupboards and onto the kitchen floor. The glass jars crashed with such force that they sent the contents across the room, with the juice hitting the ceiling. The kitchen walls and ceiling resembled a gigantic, colourful, abstract work of art with the red beetroot, green gherkin, and orangey, yellow pickles. During the next six hours, we had four more aftershocks, measuring mag. 5 or more. It was several weeks before they settled.

Between tremors, I went outside where I heard a neighbour lamenting the destruction of her crystal set. My other neighbour was frantically trying to rescue little fish that were flopping around on the lounge floor. Her large glass aquarium had fallen over and was also smashed to pieces. We were all in shock at the destruction around us. Because the pulp and paper mill close by used toxic chemicals, we were evacuated to suburbs further away. Many houses in our town had damage to their chimneys, which were later removed by the fire department.

Wives were fearful of their husband's safety at the mill, and also for the children at school. I released the boys' safety into God's hands recognizing I couldn't get to them both. Eventually, we made our way up to our large church building, which was large enough for many families to camp within. It was very eerie throughout the night trying to sleep, only to be shaken forcibly as new tremors shook the ground underneath us. It was a frightening situation for most of the children, so we all stayed close together day and night until the strong aftershocks subsided. While all this was happening, I was also trying to process my broken engagement, of which many people were unaware. The internal pressure and turmoil was a lot to handle at the same time as trying to keep my family safe. For a few nights, we moved to a friend's house where Sophie, Trev, and their children were also staying. It provided a measure of comfort and support for us to all be together, but as the tremors began to subside I decided to move back home so we could start to get back to normal.

Lying in my bed I would watch the ornaments on my shelf to see if they just wobbled or were about to fall, at which point I would call out to the boys to evacuate. Thankfully the worst was over, even though the strong tremors continued for several days. Miraculously, no one was killed. The quake was so violent that it had caused a loaded logging truck and two milk tankers to topple over. At the distillery, tanks of vodka and gin collapsed, saturating the ground in spirits. At the local pulp and paper mill, one man was trapped under eleven sharp circular saws. Miraculously, he was unhurt. One poor chap had to endure the entire earthquake swaying high in the air as he was stuck in a cheery-picker type machine!

Once everything calmed down, I was impatient to head out to Raglan so I could face Alan and bring closure. I was in turmoil over the situation. This made the two months waiting period feel like forever. Unfortunately, the earthquake had caused some huge earth slips onto the main road leading out of our town, forcing me to wait until the rocks, soil, and debris were cleared off the road.

One day in desperation I prayed and asked God if Alan was seeking Him. As I sat quietly I sensed that he wasn't, so I made plans to borrow a car and drive down to Raglan. When I rang the camp leaders, they were shocked and saddened by the situation. The camp caretakers knew what had happened and had agreed to invite Alan up without telling him I would be there. Everyone he worked with was as perplexed as I was at his behaviour. Their compassion and support meant a lot to me during those weeks. Finally, the blocked road was cleared for traffic, so I re-wrapped all the lovely engagement presents and wrote people's names on them for Alan to return them. I had placed my beautiful, expensive engagement ring in its velvet box weeks before. Once everything was loaded into the car, I began the journey to Raglan feeling vulnerable, alone, and nervous about the meeting with Alan.

Thankfully, when I arrived there was time for a nap to steady my nerves. When the caretaker came to tell me Alan was there, I wished I could have stayed in bed, blocking out the unpleasant meeting I needed to have with him. Of course, Alan looked surprised and uncomfortable when he saw me, but I suddenly felt very clear about what I needed to do. When I said we needed to talk, he suggested we drive to the beach. The atmosphere in the car was strained and awkward. I knew Alan didn't want to spend time with me, so I decided to be straight and get it over with. I told him that he had a problem with women and even though I had forgiven him for hurting me, I wanted us to end the relationship properly. He asked me what I meant. I replied that I wanted to return the engagement presents to his friends and to give him the ring back. He looked sheepish and asked me what he was supposed to do with the ring. I didn't care what happened to it, but being practical, I suggested that he sold it and paid some bills! His lack of concern, apology, or any type of explanation began to annoy me so much that I just wanted to get away from him.

Once back at the house I handed over the presents and engagement ring. Alan escaped as quickly as he could, while I stayed and had dinner with the caretakers. The whole experience of the past several weeks finally caught up with me and I went to bed emotionally exhausted. I had originally planned to drive back home the following morning, but I felt flattened, so I rested instead. A week after I returned home, I sensed God telling me that I wouldn't see Alan again, and I never did.

Looking Back

Several years later, I heard that Alan had been taken to court by one of his foster sons, who accused him of sexual abuse. After hearing a second boy share about his harrowing experience with Alan, I realised that his preference for children was why I sensed that he had a problem with women. A family friend of his told me later that Alan had also been abused as a child. As an adult, he repeated that behaviour, causing immeasurable suffering to many innocent and vulnerable children. I am incredibly grateful that I challenged him early on in our relationship, causing him to break up with me. Thank God he didn't become part of our family!

At the time of our breakup, Alan's leaders removed him from all involvement at the camps, even though no one suspected that he was abusing the children that came to him for counselling. I sincerely hope and pray that as the children got older, they confided in someone and obtained counselling from a safe, wise, compassionate person.

CHAPTER TWELVE

Release

1988

The broken engagement had left me with a deep sense of rejection. I felt empty inside, with little interest in being with people. Swimming and working in the garden became my places of solace during this season of healing.

Then God began to guide me in a fresh direction through a book called *Is That Really You God?* by Loren Cunningham. Loren was the founder of Youth With A Mission (YWAM), an international organization that disciples young people and takes them on outreaches. As I read his incredible journey of sensing God's heartbeat for the lost and taking teams of youth to different people groups, a fresh longing began to rise within me. For some time, I had been feeling trapped in an endless cycle of church meetings and activity that now drained me. My heart was no longer content with the familiar routines of the past five years.

Upon reading Loren's book, a desire to pursue the calling to Africa began to grow again. I contacted YWAM in Auckland to send me the application papers for their discipleship training course, but when I saw that Pastor Tom would have to sign the form, my heart sank; I knew he was not supportive of my calling. One Sunday, in the middle of a message, he had remarked snidely about "people who want to run away to Africa." I felt mocked and belittled in front of the congregation. After several nights of broken sleep, agonizing over how to approach him and how to get to YWAM if he said no, I couldn't stand the suspense any longer so I made an appointment to see him that week. His wife Pam was a gentle and empathetic person. I knew she would understand my request, but she would support her husband's decision.

Once I shared my vision and the application forms with Tom, he spoke very bluntly to me and then adamantly refused to sign. Pam hugged me with a sad look on her face as they left. From that time onwards, I endured church, but felt like an outsider. It was a lonely time for me, but I continued praying and trusting God for a breakthrough. Then to my surprise, God did something very unusual to vindicate and release me. He knew I would not leave my church fellowship, no matter how miserable I felt, until He specifically told me to.

In mid-1988, our church invited a team of pastors from out of town to spend the weekend prophesying over each person. This was a regular event that brought great encouragement to us all. During the Sunday morning service, one of the visiting pastors stopped preaching in the middle of his message and pointed at me. In a clear, loud voice he said, "The Lord had shown me that you are discouraged, frustrated, and depressed." I began crying, as it was all true. Then he said with authority, "The Lord is releasing you TODAY!" A huge oppressive weight lifted off me and I began to sob deeply while someone held me. It was over! The constant feeling of being disobedient and out of step with everyone else that had brought great loneliness and shame into my life was ending. The result of that clear insight spoken publicly was that I felt understood, vindicated, and affirmed by God Himself. I was now free to find another place to worship and pursue my vision to train in Africa with YWAM.

Aware of how difficult it had been for me at this church, the assistant pastors, Denise and Joe, told me they supported my decision. After asking God which church I was to move to, my attention was drawn towards the Salvation Army church across the road from our home. The next Sunday morning, as I walked there with the boys, I was feeling very apprehensive. I asked God, "Is this you leading me? Please don't let me make a mistake. I need you to confirm that I am doing the right thing."

Once inside the building, I was relieved to discover warm, friendly people who worshipped enthusiastically. The Captain/pastor welcomed us and then gave a passionate and sincere message which touched my heart. After the service, several people came over to introduce themselves. I returned home full of joy and gratitude at God's faithfulness. He had led me to a group of vibrant believers. Having decided the Salvation Army would be our new spiritual home, I wrote a letter to Pastor Tom, asking to be released from the CCF so we could move to the Salvation Army. I felt it was important to return one last Sunday to be prayed over properly.

Two days later, Denise rang to say that Tom wanted me to meet with the leadership team one evening. I immediately felt nervous. I knew Denise was supportive, but what about Joe, her husband? She assured me that he also recognised that God had released me. With this in mind, I agreed and they gave me a ride to the meeting two nights later. The two pastors, their wives, and I were the only people present. Little did I realise that I was about to face two hours of questions and accusations.

When I said that I was moving to the Salvation Army, they told me that I would die spiritually there. That made me angry. I replied that I wouldn't because the believers there loved the Lord passionately. When I raised the issue of being prayed for on Sunday to release me, Tom stated they wouldn't do that. Even when I said that I needed the boys to see me doing things the right way, they still refused.

I was at a loss for words. Joe had not been at all supportive, but rather had joined in the criticism. I felt conned into coming to what now felt like a verbal assault. Feeling trapped and thoroughly told off, I looked at Pam, who was sitting quietly with a sad look on her face. I knew she was upset at the harshness towards me. Denise, who was more vocal, was angry and argued about different points. She reminded the men that God had sent a visiting pastor to declare publicly that He was releasing me. I was grateful for her support, but the men wouldn't budge. We drove home in an uncomfortable atmosphere, with Denise reminding Joe of his promise to be supportive and upset that he hadn't kept his word. I just wanted to go home and be left alone.

It had been a lonely and tiring two hours for me, but what I had just encountered had only served to confirm to me that I had made the right decision by leaving. Over the next several weeks, I was shunned by most members of the church. One person told me later that they were told I had left in disobedience. As we lived in a small town, it was natural to see each other regularly at the shops, the bank, and also when picking up our kids each day at the local schools. My former friends looked very uncomfortable and quickly turned away without speaking to me. My younger sister Sophie, who usually rang me most days, didn't do so for five weeks. This hurt very deeply, but I understood the position she was in, as the pastor's word was law and the congregation were supposed to be obedient. In some churches in those days, if a woman questioned or disagreed with a leader's decision, she would often be accused of having a rebellious spirit. Men were the "priests" of the home and had the final say on most things. Many women were silenced and their giftings ignored during this era.

I forgave Tom and Joe but was so hurt that I became critical towards them. Unfortunately, anger and self-pity were my companions for quite some time. Years later, Tom and I reconciled and apologised to each other. This laid the foundation for a more relaxed relationship.

At the Salvation Army, I made wonderful friends, some of whom had been through similar trials to my own. One special friend was Gillian, who had a great sense of humour and a loud laugh like a machine gun! Her humour was a tonic to me. In August, I became concerned for her due to a specific situation, so I began to fast and pray. During the weeks of fasting, I learnt about the importance of not being critical and judgmental, but instead to give unconditional love to people in my life. James 2:13, "Mercy triumphs over judgment" (NIV) became very real to me.

One day, when I felt particularly concerned for Gillian, I rang her. When she didn't reply, I biked to her place, opened the front door, and called out. There was silence. Instead of going home, I felt prompted to go to her bedroom, where I looked behind the door. To my shock, I saw Gillian hiding there and immediately realised that she hadn't wanted to see me. It was an awkward moment because she just stared at me without saying anything, so I joined her behind the door and then wondered what the heck I should say. After a few minutes of looking at each other in silence I said, "Shall we go and have a cuppa?" Gillian reminded me recently about that crazy event, thirty years ago, where God had led me straight to her hiding place! He knew she was isolating herself from people at a time when a friend to talk with was what she needed most.

At church, I was asked to lead the Sunday School and to train the teachers. I had recently discovered some wonderful musical plays for children's groups, so I sent to America for one. Each of the Sunday School classes was allocated a song that they were to express creatively with either tambourines, dance, ribbons, puppets, or acting. An older child would narrate the story in between each musical item. This was to become our Christmas pageant, presented in November to family and friends. The children worked hard and presented two wonderful pageants to enthusiastic audiences. Doing something different and creative had been great fun for us all. A difficult year had ended on a high note.

In early December I had a sense of God saying to me, "Chris you have done what I asked you to do (focus on being a Mum), and you've done a good job." My immediate reaction was, "Gosh, Lord, is our time in Coniston coming to an end?" I certainly felt ready for something new.

My friend Bev was on the board of Women's Aglow and had invited me to be the end-of-year guest speaker. My theme was the "Father Heart of God." I loved speaking about my tender, kind, merciful, forgiving Father whose love had sustained and healed me during the most difficult times. I emphasised that our walk with Him was about love and acceptance, not performance or control. Control crushes, whereas love releases. Afterwards, several women came forward to be ministered to.

Once the boys' schools closed for the seven week Christmas holidays, I became aware of feeling physically trapped in our small town. Without a car, we could not get out and about, which meant the boys were restless and bored. In January, God nudged my sister Margy to ring me and find out how we were all doing. After explaining the situation to her, she immediately sent money for Joshua to fly to his beloved Nana in Christchurch. Josh loved the feeling of freedom he got from being in a city, where he could explore and do interesting things. I could see he was excited to be spreading his wings a bit. My mother looked forward to his arrival, especially after the recent death of Dad's mother, our adored Nana. Each day Mum would walk to Nana's flat to spend a few hours with her, and was now feeling her loss acutely. How wonderful that God had made a way for Mum to have the company of a vibrant, inquisitive, young lad. I knew they would have a great time together.

Eli and I took a bus to Auckland and had a wonderful holiday with Margy and her family. We were both excited on the trip up, as we knew Margy and Fred would spoil us and take us out most days. They were incredibly generous to many people. A bonus for me was that I could switch off to all the endless responsibilities and simply relax for a while with the companionship of my precious sister. Sheer bliss!

Pastor George - a man of the Word

**Pastor George and Wyn Ehau of Faith Family Fellowship -
Aranui / Wainoni**

CHAPTER THIRTEEN

A Pivotal Meeting

JANUARY 1990

At this point, I had been raising my sons on my own while being involved in all types of children's ministries and working in a difficult environment as a relief teacher at the local schools. The thought of doing all these demanding roles for another year made my heart sink. I kept thinking, "There must be more to this Christian walk than just attending services every week, helping with Sunday school, and going to the occasional mission's conference."

The truth was that I was feeling discontented, bored, and stagnant. At a recent missions conference, I was gripped once again by a longing to minister to the lost. Reading the New Testament, I hungered to belong to a mature community of believers whose focus was on living in the reality of Jesus's lifestyle, which included sacrificial service to those in need. Instead, I kept bumping up against church politics and believers who saw the mission field as a destination for a select few.

I realised I was slowly dying inside. Something needed to change!

Then, my dear Anglican friends Bev and Ian Robertson invited me to join them at a "Rise Up" conference in Rotorua. Jackie Pullinger and John Dawson (a YWAM leader) were the main speakers. Since Jackie was one of my heroines of the faith, I was keen to go. She was an English girl with a degree in music who sold everything she owned and bought a ticket to Hong Kong. Once there, Jackie began to minister to drug addicts in the "walled city"—a secret place within Hong Kong full of gangsters and opium dens. Jackie prayed in tongues, while the addicts lay sweating on mats as they kicked their drug habit. She shared her flat with those in need and lived a simple life. Jackie's life was one of great sacrifice to the neediest people around her, the poorest of the poor. Years before, I had bought a book about her ministry. It was an incredible story of courage, passion, and obedience. God protected her daily in dangerous situations.

At the time I attended the conference, I felt dull in my spirit and was probably a bit depressed. Jackie was blunt and challenged everyone to get moving! In her forthright manner, she declared, "You are a light and need to go to a dark place. You are not meant to cling to a comfortable way of life."

"Here is my 'fruit,'" she said, pointing to the front row, where a group of ex-addicts from Hong Kong sat. "Where is your fruit?" Many of us shifted uncomfortably in our seats and shrunk in stature at the rawness of this challenge, but the point was driven home. Where was our fruit, from our cosy predictable lives? I heartily agreed with her but was also deeply challenged.

Once the conference ended, the hall quickly emptied. I sat near the front, waiting for Bev and Ian to finish talking with an old friend. I had told God the night before that I felt like I was at a dead end. I was a pioneer who thrived on new challenges and the sameness of the past five years had worn me down. I had come to the conference hoping to receive a personal word that would revive me and guide me through the coming year. With all the struggles and disappointments over the years, I had lost my first love for Jesus. This deeply concerned me.

Deep in thought, I happened to glance up and was surprised to see John Dawson walking across the stage and down the steps to the auditorium. I immediately jumped out of my seat as I knew this was a God-given opportunity to share my heart with a YWAM leader. I briefly told him of my calling to Africa and the ten years of proving myself at each church by being actively involved in children's ministry. In frustration, I blurted out, "I am tired of jumping through hoops for man. I know I am meant to be in Africa!"

He surprised me by saying "Then just go." I asked John where I should go, and he replied that because South Africa had the best training base in Africa, I should apply there. He then looked me straight in the eye and said, "Chris, I am the leader of a large base in Los Angeles and have many people on staff. I have written several books and often travel internationally. I want you to know that I am proud of you, for persevering in this missions calling." Tears came to my eyes as these powerful words from a wise, sensitive man of God flowed over me. It was like healing balm was being applied to my battered soul. Fresh determination and courage rose within. I felt restored and valuable again. Oh, the power of life-giving words!

John prayed, then asked me to write to him in six months to let him know what was happening. He ended with, "I have a spiritual interest in you now Chris." I was absolutely elated at this last-minute encounter. It had built me up so much and given me clear direction. God had faithfully and powerfully answered the cry of my heart for a personal word of direction.

Once I was back home, a major battle began within my soul. Fear of rejection and the possibility of failure gripped me as I contemplated beginning the process of contacting YWAM. After much crying and telling God that I couldn't stand it if they refused to train me, I finally rang South Africa to request the application forms. This was no longer just a dream. I was beginning on a journey which would require us to leave everything and everyone we had ever known and travel halfway around the world. We would be living in a foreign culture where we knew no one. If it had just been me going alone, I would have done so without hesitation, but being responsible for the two boys significantly changed the dynamics of emigrating. I couldn't afford to make any big mistakes and risk hurting them.

That week, I realised that I was already feeling defeated! So much of the earlier fire, courage, and strength had been eroded through fear. As I walked to town, a car pulled up to the kerb beside me. The driver was Pastor Ray Coffin, a speaker at some Women's Aglow meetings. He asked me how I was doing, and when I told him he said, "It is the end of one vision and the start of another, which at this stage is still vague, but unfolding." Sharing my concern about the possibility of not being accepted by YWAM, Ray replied, "You need a good dose of determination to see this through." I was grateful that God had sent him to encourage me just when I needed it. Pondering on Ray's words, I made a simple plan. If YWAM South Africa denied my application, then I would immediately apply to YWAM in New Zealand. I was not going to give up easily!

Josh was enjoying his time with Mum, getting out and about in Christchurch. I knew he wanted to stay in New Zealand and that he was hoping to board with Mum while he finished secondary school but when I asked her, she said she couldn't. This was disappointing but understandable; being responsible for a teen age boy is not always easy. To soften the blow, Mum bought Josh a computer, which for him was as wonderful as winning the lottery. Josh was ecstatic because he now had an opportunity to teach himself some new skills.

At the end of March, Josh moved to the Baptist church to join their vibrant youth group. Every Friday afternoon, Andrew, the youth leader, drove around our town collecting the members of the youth group in his van. Josh made some good friends there and had many a fun evening with them all. In the Salvation Army, he had been faithfully playing the drums at both the morning and evening services on Sundays, but with only one other boy his age there, it was a lonely place for him.

I was still at the Salvation Army, but the sense of acceptance and joy had erroded over time. The previous year, several people had left the church due to feeling criticised and intimidated by the Captain's wife. She was quite abrupt when correcting people. Some wanted to discuss what they were experiencing with me, but I was uncomfortable being put in that position. I knew their distress was real, but I was nervous about becoming involved in church politics again. I slowly eased myself out of all church responsibilities, which included resigning from leading the Sunday School. With all the unrest and criticism taking place, I had lost interest and felt like I was just going through the motions. It was time to step down and allow someone else with a fresh vision and passion to lead this important work.

Nevertheless, our leader, Captain Pete, was a warm, spirit-filled man who I respected and appreciated. He was supportive of my going to YWAM and willingly signed the papers when they arrived from South Africa. My focus now was on preparing the boys for the big move ahead of us.

After my chance encounter with Pastor Ray telling me that I needed to have a good dose of determination, God highlighted a particular scripture to me which I wrote out on a large strip of cardboard and stuck on my bedroom wall. It was from Psalm 84, verse 11b, "No good thing does He withhold from those whose walk is blameless" (NIV). My part was to walk uprightly with God so that He could release all the good things He had for me, and I was determined to do my part. I could then rest in the knowledge that God would provide everything we would need. This included the house selling at the right time for a good price.

When I rang Ray to discuss this verse he asked me if there was any unrighteousness in my life. After some soul searching, I could confidently say that the only thing that came to mind was the need for me to watch my attitude towards leaders, especially when I saw people being hurt by their harsh words. The tense atmosphere at church was making me anxious, so I spoke with an elder to ask for his advice. He had also been aware of what was happening and suggested that a few of us meet with Captain Pete and then share our concerns with him together.

Later, as I spent time seeking God, I felt He directed me to "go as a friend and speak the truth." I reminded myself that God desires truth in our innermost being, so I rang Pete for an appointment. As I walked over to their house, I felt calm because I had a good relationship with Pete and I had found him to be a reasonable man. Also, my goal was for reconciliation between leadership and those who had left or were on the verge of leaving. As an optimist, I believed that this was possible. The reality, however, was quite different. Joy sat next to me on the couch, which threw me off track initially, as I had hoped to speak with Pete alone. Gathering courage, and praying for wisdom I began by asking him if he had noticed that we were losing people in our fellowship, to which he replied "No." Gulp! This wasn't going to be easy.

I tried again and said that several people had come to me for counselling as they were finding it hard to cope at church and were seriously thinking about leaving. By now, I was wishing I hadn't made this appointment, painfully aware of Joy beside me. How could I explain that her behaviour was hurting people and causing them to leave? Pete was looking expectantly at me, so I sent up a quick prayer for courage, then told them the truth as gently as I could. Pete disagreed that there was a problem with people leaving, so I thanked them for their time and walked home feeling ghastly.

The fact that this was their first posting as pastors weighed heavily on my mind as I walked home. I didn't want to be a source of discouragement to them. Making them feel like failures was a horrible and unintended possibility. My goal had been to give them some insight and to encourage reconciliation. I said to God, "Don't ever ask me to do something like that again." It had been a miserable experience, which then made me anxious all evening. I had obviously got it all wrong!

Early the next morning there was a knock on the door. Captain Pete asked me if he could come in and then began to share an encounter he had with God during the night. God had woken him and shown him the faces of people who had been hurt. He apologised to me, and then said that he planned to apologise to the congregation on Sunday morning. I felt an immense sense of relief, as well as a deep respect for his humility. I played a song for him that God had brought to my mind the day before when I was preparing to meet with him. It was entitled, "He Who Began a Good Work in You." It was an encouraging song about God being committed to completing what He had begun in each of us. Pete thanked me, then returned home. My desire was that his wife was also going to be as open and humble as he was, allowing the healing process for our fellowship to begin. Sadly, this didn't happen. On Sunday, Pete spoke briefly, apologised, then began playing the piano for our worship time.

Two key people wrote letters to the leaders explaining how they had been hurt and shut down, then they left. Where once we had been a vibrant, passionate, joy-filled congregation, the atmosphere in our meetings was now clogged with heavy sadness, distrust, and hurts that had not been dealt with. I just wanted to stay at home now.

In mid-March I rang YWAM South Africa to ask if my application had been processed. The receptionist said she would ask the leaders of the Crossroads School (for older students) to ring me back. Two weeks later, when they still hadn't called back, I became impatient; I knew my season in Coniston was coming to an end. Even if YWAM didn't accept me, I had decided we would go to Africa regardless and trust God to open another door. It all felt quite surreal and daunting, but a change was in the air! Eli had been speaking with his father in Zimbabwe and was understandably keen to live closer to him and his two younger siblings.

My only desire now was to head for Africa and trust God to guide and provide for us. One evening, while I was lying on the couch processing the enormous responsibility I felt for leaving New Zealand with my sons, the phone rang. It was a friend who said, "Chris, I was making tea when I had a strong urge that I had to ring you and say that you may have two boys with you on your journey, but Moses was told to leave Egypt and set off for an unknown destination with three million people. So what if you have two boys with you! God will lead the way." I was stunned at the timing of this encouraging message to me from someone who was totally unaware of what I was privately processing at that exact moment! That short phone call was God reassuring me that

I was doing the right thing.

 My next move was to call a real estate agent to value our home, which I then put on the market. From that moment onwards, it was like being on a gigantic emotional roller coaster ride. At times I was decisive and at others I wobbled. After a few people had commented that I was making a big mistake, I once again began to doubt what I was doing and slowly my resolve weakened. Confusion robbed me of my former determination. I had no one with missions experience to turn to when I was feeling battered with negative comments. During the first half of 1989, I repeatedly lost ground, and then rose again as Bev and other friends encouraged me. Mentally and emotionally, it was an exhausting process.

However, as I reflected on when I had lost my peace about emigrating, I realised it was when I took notice of the negative comments. I had let them chip away at my confidence, which resulted in me becoming unsure. God's Word states that, "He has not given us a spirit of fear but of power and love and a sound mind" (2 Tim. 1:7, NKJV). I knew the confusion was not from Him. A quote from V. Raymond Edmund helped me to keep focusing on the vision God had given me ten years before: "Don't doubt in the darkness what God has shown you in the light."

I was learning that everyone had an opinion and sometimes they gave advice that they thought would be helpful, but often wasn't. They didn't have God's perspective for my life. I am sure that Peter would not have gotten out of the boat and walked on water if he had first decided to ask all the other disciples what they thought about his chances of sinking. I was discovering that obeying God's calling could be very lonely at times; being misunderstood seemed to be a part of the process. With all this in mind, I embraced God's instructions to me, learning the important lesson of guarding my mind. Once again I felt steady, confident, and at peace.

While I knew I was doing the right thing, it was still very sobering to put our home up for sale. This was the point of no return. I was truly committed in every way to dismantling our life in Coniston. One of the thoughts that occasionally came to my mind was that it might not work out as I had hoped once we were in Africa. After all, I had never travelled outside of New Zealand. I had no experience of living in another country and culture.

Then I remembered an article that I had read in the Reader's Digest magazine years before. It stated that when you were faced with the unknown, it was important to ask yourself two questions. The first was, "What is the worst that could happen?" I thought about this and decided that the worst thing that could happen would be if, after attending the first course in South Africa, we ran out of money. This would mean returning to New Zealand where we would no longer have a home to which to return.

The second question was, "Could you handle this?" After pondering this question my answer was a big "Yes." We would move to Auckland, near Margy, rent a flat and gradually get established again. This way I wouldn't need to face anyone in Coniston, letting them know that my big venture had failed! With a buoyant heart that was now confident that I could face the worst scenario, I said to myself, "Besides, I would be the only person in our street who had ever been to Africa!" This new perspective made me smile! Once again the anticipation of this daring new venture surged through me, bringing joy and fresh determination. Now I just had to wait for the house to sell.

In May I rang YWAM again, as I still hadn't heard from them regarding my application. A few weeks later, I received confirmation that I had been accepted for the August discipleship school. I was ecstatic and rearing to go. The letter described the seaside town we would be living in while I trained. A second letter was for the South African Embassy in Sydney, where I would need to apply for study visas.

In August, when the house still had not sold, I rang the school leaders to tell them that I couldn't make it for the August school, and suggested that I came instead to the next Crossroads school in January. I was shocked to learn that the Crossroads schools were only being held once a year, due to the shortage of staff. Cheryl, the leader, told me the next school was in January, but it was five months long and for younger people. In my heart, I had felt all along that we would arrive in January, as I planned to travel to Australia and England in December after we sold the house.

When I told Cheryl that I was happy to be on the January school, she asked me to ring nearer the Crossroads starting date, August 10th, to confirm if I was still not able to make it. I began to fast and pray, asking God to close the wrong door and open the right one for me. To my consternation, the house was still not selling! Once again I became anxious as the school leaders were keen for me to come. I felt that they were mature, experienced missionaries, who knew God's voice better than me.

When I rang them on August 10th to say I wasn't coming, they said that they were in a meeting where they had been praying for a miracle for us, and again asked me to ring back if our situation changed. The school leaders believed that I was meant to be in South Africa by mid-August. Their certainty caused me to became anxious and confused. Was my faith too small? Was I holding things up? I felt sick in my stomach as I tried to work out the reason for the delay. The visa papers from Sydney had not arrived back yet, which caused me to agonize more. "Lord, what if someone buys the house for cash in the next three weeks and I don't have the visas? This could mess up your plans for us!" The internal pressure I felt was enormous.

Slowly, I began to realise that I was looking more to leaders to tell me what was right instead of letting God guide us by opening the right door at the right time. Yes, they were more experienced missionaries than me, but God had led me this far and He would continue to do so. With this in mind, my peace steadily returned.

The school leader rang to ask if there had been a change. When I replied in the negative, he said that if I wasn't at the August school, it would feel like a key person was missing. Having released myself from the time pressure, I was able to calmly thank him for his encouragement and tell him that after I had fasted and prayed again, I was now content to aim for the January school for younger people. When the August school began, I thought of them all, but was totally at peace, safe in the knowledge that God knew the right timing for everything.

Over ten years had passed since I had organized a passport for my journey to Africa. As they are only valid for ten years my new unused passport had expired and I had to apply for a new one. A few days later the visa application papers and study permit forms arrived from Sydney, which Bev helped me complete.

Meanwhile, I began ringing shipping companies to get a quote for sending boxes with our linen, kitchenware and the boys favourite books and toys to South Africa. The price was so high that I realised I needed to sell or give away most of our belongings. Thus began a huge process of deciding what to do with every item in the house. Margy offered to store some boxes at her home until we got settled and they could be sent to us.

My precious friends from the early Salvation Army days and Bev and Pam from my former church all encouraged me during this time. Pam told me I was ready to go. Ray Coffin rang to enquire how things were shaping up. His advice to me was to ask God why the house hadn't sold yet, in case there was a blockage. If not, then speak confidently, not out of insecurity! He was right of course. My words needed to align with God's promises to me.

One of Josh's college teachers was a man from South Africa who had grown up in the apartheid era. In South Africa he had been classed as a "coloured person." His insights and tales of life there painted a very negative picture. This affected Josh a lot. When I rang Eli's father to tell him that we were moving to South Africa, he was shocked because he was well aware of the unjust system which oppressed the black and coloured communities there. However, once he realised that Eli would be living closer to him, he promptly invited Eli for a holiday with his family in Zimbabwe before going to South Africa.

The airlines informed me that all the flights for December and early January were full, so I booked Eli on standby, praying that someone would cancel their booking. Next, I contacted my brother in England to ask if we could stay with them after visiting Australia. Organizing our travel itinerary was great fun as I began to imagine us all travelling around the world. It was very surreal!

A book called *Power in Praise* by Merlin Carothers was a great motivator at this time. I needed to build trust and confidence in God's abilities and not my own. I had spent too much time agonizing, fretting, and trying to work everything out. This had only left me feeling quite unwell in the past. A key was to declare God's promises in every situation. This would help to keep me strong and focused. Around this time, 1 John 5:14-15 gave me deep insight: "Now this is the confidence that we have in Him, that if we ask anything according to His will, He hears us. And if we know that He hears us, whatever we ask, we know that we have the petitions that we have asked of Him" (NKJV). The key was to make sure that our requests were in agreement with His plans!

Bev told me that our soul—the mind, will, and emotions—has had control for so long that it doesn't want to release control to the Holy Spirit. Our will decides who will dominate: the soul or the Holy Spirit. The Holy Spirit's leading will always line up with the Word of God. Having spent years repenting of criticism, fault-finding, and anger at people, I was looking forward to the day when the Holy Spirit was the one leading the way in my thoughts and actions. It had been a relentless battle so far. I noticed it was so easy to see other people's faults while remaining blind to my own!

"Lord, I need your help in these areas," I prayed.

A book I was reading by Fred Renich, *When the Chisel Hits the Rock*, shed some much needed light on what God had been doing with me as I prepared for the mission field. It described the preparation process that takes place between receiving God's vision and the actual fulfilment. Renich says that God makes us into the person who will carry out His vision for our lives, but we don't always start that way. The process of being moulded and "chiselled" can be a long and painful one, but one that ultimately leads to our sanctification and the fulfilment of God's plan for our lives. Reading that made me realise that God had been chiselling me all along, and the experiences I had that were painful or the time it took to get to the place I was then, was all a part of His plan, of him making me into the person with the kind of character who could carry out His call on my life.

Looking Back

I found this book had profound truths that I didn't fully understand at the time. At age 67, as I look back over my life, particularly the twenty-four years in Africa, I am acutely aware of the importance of Godly character. The loving heart of our Heavenly Father is the motivation behind all the valleys we go through. In them, with Him, we are moulded and shaped into vessels of honour that carry His presence wherever we go.

CHAPTER FOURTEEN

The Final Stretch in New Zealand

OCTOBER - DECEMBER 1990

The house had been on the market for several months with no sale in sight, and the end of the year was approaching. I had made plans for us to travel to Australia in December, meaning it was imperative that the house sold quickly. During this time I was on edge, waiting for a breakthrough as so much depended on finances being freed up.

Then, the house sold! Oh, the relief that flooded my soul! Now we could complete the travel itinerary and pay to book our flights. After such a long tumultuous time, things finally seemed to be falling into place; we would now make it to the January Discipleship Training School (D.T.S) after all.

The next two weeks were a whirl of activity as we packed up what was coming with us and disposed of everything else. Bev and Ian had invited us to stay with them for three weeks while Josh sat his School Certificate, which is a national exam. I was fortunate to have Bev for a mentor, counsellor, and close friend during the six years we lived in Coniston. The night before Josh was due to sit his science exam, he complained of a sore throat and headaches. I noticed his eyes were a bright red and asked Bev to take a look. "Look at that rash!" she exclaimed. "Does he have measles?"

Surely not! But when he lifted his shirt we saw a rash all over his torso. Poor lad! Just as he's about to sit his final exams and we are due to fly out of New Zealand, he develops measles. At 9 a.m. I took him to the doctor who confirmed it was measles and instructed me to quarantine him at home. After a routine blood test, Joshua felt quite weak and promptly went to sleep. I rang the school to explain what had happened to him and dropped a doctor's certificate off. He would be staying home for several days to recover, which meant he couldn't come on the celebration outing with Eli and I that we had all been looking forward to. We invited Archie, a friend of Eli's, along to keep Eli company instead.

Bev and Ian travelled to their holiday cottage at Whangamata while I took Eli and Archie to Leisure World in Rotorua. While the boys had a fun time on the hydro slide and other rides, I went for a walk to a pond to watch the swans gliding elegantly around the lake.

After chatting with an American couple who were enjoying a trip around the world, I collected the boys for a special lunch at The International Hotel. Having a meal there had been a special treat for us as a family. Due to a tight budget, we seldom went out for a meal, except on one of our birthdays. It had become a family tradition to borrow a car so I could drive us through the forests and along the lakeside to Rotorua, where we enjoyed a delicious buffet lunch.

The first time Joshua, Eli and I went there we were stunned by the vast array of food set out artistically on several long tables. It seemed like all our Christmases had come at once. We began with large plates of seafood. Eli had three plates of prawns for an entrée, followed by roast vegetables with pork, lamb, or beef. I was full after the seafood and roast meal, but the lads were ploughing through plate after plate of food with great concentration. I decided to have a little taste of some of the delectable desserts. With my sweet tooth, desserts are my favourite part of any meal. After finishing our trifle, pastries, and ice cream, Eli surprised us by returning to the seafood section and returning with his fourth plate of prawns! Joshua and I could only stare in absolute amazement at his capacity!

We groaned at the thought of so much seafood being added to the enormous quantity of food he had already managed to pack away. The irony was that because Eli was only nine years of age, his meal only cost ten dollars, even though his entire meal consisted of three plates of prawns, two plates of roast meat and vegetables, two plates of dessert and a final plate of seafood! Joshua and I could only stare in amazement at him as he packed away so much food. I joked with Josh that they should have weighed him before we entered and again when we left, then charged him for the difference. He must have put on several kilos at least. Eli's parting comment as we left the table was, "I can't fit any more in." He looked frustrated and sad at this reality. I was not looking forward to all the twists and turns on the trip back to Coniston. The journey is a winding one, and best not done on a full stomach! Thankfully, on this final celebration meal, Eli was restrained and ate more moderately while chatting with Archie.

The reality of leaving my close friends and family was uppermost in my mind at this time. My younger sister Sophie and I had been together through most of our adult life, supporting each other emotionally, financially, and through the births and rearing of our children. I knew it would not be easy to say goodbye to her. With this in mind, I decided to return to her fellowship for the last two Sundays. After speaking with Pete and Joy, they prayed for us on our last Sunday at the Salvation Army. Sophie organized a surprise farewell party for me that had an African theme. We all dressed up in colourful clothes and enjoyed an evening of hilarious games and jokes speculating about what I would encounter. Sophie has a zany sense of humour, so it was a great evening. Being able to relax with my old friends from my former church was also very healing.

On our last weekend in Coniston, I was wondering if Pastor Tom would invite me to say something to the congregation, or if he would pray for us. This didn't happen, however, as I was sick in bed on Sunday. Sophie told me that Presbytery meetings were being held from Monday to Wednesday evenings. I had always enjoyed the experience of visiting pastors prophesying over the congregation, so I decided to attend the last meeting on Wednesday evening. As we would leave the next morning, this would give me time to farewell my friends and provide the pastors with an opportunity to pray over me and send us to Africa. Everyone was aware that this was our last evening in Coniston. Towards the end of the evening, a few people were looking concerned and whispered to me, "Ask to be prayed for Chris." I was sad that there was no desire from the leadership to acknowledge that I was leaving to train in Africa, so I decided to keep quiet. After the meeting ended, my friends and I chatted while we enjoyed a cup of tea. Surely one of the leaders would approach me to give their blessing before we left New Zealand. But this didn't happen.

As I left the building bewildered and sad, some people hugged me farewell. I saw Pastor Tom and his wife in their car. She looked sad and uncomfortable. I decided to approach them; it wasn't right to pretend nothing significant was about to happen to the lads and me. I walked up to Pastor Tom as he was about to drive away and said, "I leave for Africa next week, so I won't be seeing you again. I just wanted to say goodbye." He looked at me and said, "We are off to the promised land.

Goodbye." I knew they were moving to the Chatham Islands soon, and replied "Anywhere God sends us is the promised land. Goodbye." I made my way home with a heavy heart, aware that this was not how it ought to end!

At home, I shared with Bev and Ian what had happened and how disturbed I felt. I was crying as I spoke. It had been important to me, to end my time in New Zealand well. I believed in the spiritual principle of being "sent" by the elders. Ian offered to pray for me instead, and as he and Bev laid their hands on my head, they "sent" me to Africa with their blessings. They had, in effect, commissioned me to go to the mission field in their kitchen. Peace returned to my mind and heart again and I felt ready to leave.

As I surveyed the bedroom and lounge at Bev's, I was overwhelmed with the number of belongings that I still needed to sell or pack. Some of the boxes were to be stored at my sister Margy's home in Auckland. My brain was quite numb by now with all the hundreds of decisions I had been making, as well as the emotional turmoil of dealing with a sick son, and saying farewell to my sister and all my friends, much less contemplating taking the three of us into the vast unknown of Africa.

I had been waiting for Eli's father Solomon to send ticket money for Eli, since Eli was leaving Josh and me in Sydney to fly straight to his father in Zimbabwe. But Solomon had delayed sending it, so now I needed to also buy Eli's ticket. It was stressful waiting for the visas and study permits from the South African embassy in Sydney. They had not been granted yet. The travel agent handling all this was quite uptight with me when she rang. She mentioned placing a collect call to the embassy and adding the cost to my bill. Bill? I didn't realise I would have a bill from her. Having never travelled internationally before, I was ignorant of quite a lot of details and procedures, which made me feel insecure.

Bev was concerned we wouldn't be ready by the next morning, when my close friend Viv would collect us in her car and drive us up to Margy's. Looking at the increasing number of boxes and bags, I was concerned that we wouldn't fit all the luggage into her car, so I rang the Intercity Bus Company to enquire about the cost of freight, but discovered it was too expensive to consider as an option. Finally, I rang Viv to say we couldn't go with her due to the large amount of luggage we had. Viv is a very resourceful woman who quickly organized a van and a trailer from The Ark, the organization for which she worked. Viv commented that she hoped we didn't mind travelling in a van with a rainbow on the side and a large giraffe painted on the front. Eli was indignant and declared he wouldn't be travelling in any vehicle with rainbows and giraffes on it!

On our last evening in Coniston, I felt drained from the pressure of finalizing everything, last-minute packing, and spending time with my friends who came to say goodbye. There was still so much to be done. Although I was exhausted, at 1:30am I was still busy sewing some modest cotton dresses that would be culturally appropriate. Bev kept me company, gluing a family photo she had taken onto support cards that we intended giving to friends and family to remind them to pray for us.

After only a few hours' sleep, I was up early to continue getting us ready for Viv's arrival. She very capably packed all our boxes and bags into the trailer and van. Having had years of camping experience with her family, she was the right person to handle this task. I was hardly able to think straight at this point due to all the stress I was feeling. Eli was relieved to discover the van only had a tiny Ark sign on the side with no giraffe in sight. He sat in the back seat with his close friend Archie—who was more like a brother to him—enjoying their last moments together. I cried as we said a final goodbye to Archie; after so many weekends and holidays at our home over the years, he felt like my son. Joshua was staying behind to attend a Baptist Youth camp that weekend, but I knew it would also be difficult for him to leave his close friends behind.

Finally, it was time to leave. We drove off waving to Ian and Bev who had been a tower of strength and support to me all the years we had lived in Coniston.

The journey to Auckland took several hours, which allowed me to unwind as Viv and I chatted. We stopped for lunch along the way, enjoying the peace of finally being able to relax from the weeks of hectic activity. It was late afternoon when we arrived at my sister Margy's lovely spacious home in the countryside. The knowledge that we no longer had a home of our own felt very surreal at that moment. I kept checking with the travel agent to see if our visas had been granted. Both of us were shocked when she received the news that they had been denied. This was a serious blow; I couldn't enter South Africa without them. As I prayed, I wondered what was happening and how to proceed.

Josh arrived back from camp by bus in time for three fun days of shopping for presents at the huge malls. The next day, Sophie and her family joined us in time for an early Christmas celebration together. We were all aware that this would possibly be our last Christmas together for many years. Despite the joy of all being together, I was very aware that the days were disappearing in a flurry of last minute preparations.

Mum was naturally anxious for us as I had sold our family home and was taking her grandsons to a distant and controversial country in Africa. This was very hard for her to process because her priority was our safety. As Mum and Margy talked, they expressed their concerns about how icy cold it was in England at this time of year. They were also both naturally anxious that the visas had been denied. I was equally concerned, but at this point, I could only trust God to intervene and make a way for us to enter South Africa to study. I had been through many difficulties in my life and had learned to overcome them with God's help. With my characteristic positivity and make-a-new-plan attitude, I was determined to keep moving forward, trusting that God would sort out the visa situation along the way. My family, understandably, probably thought I was in denial and was being reckless. They were very concerned about our situation and kept discussing it which made me feel drained and anxious. The next day we visited my mother's cousin, Aunty Marea, who began to panic when she heard about the lack of visas. She insisted on ringing Qantas airlines as she had heard they were about to go on strike! After she rebuked me for my airy-fairy attitude, I was desperate to leave everyone and spend some time alone. All their anxiety and panic was becoming too stressful for me.

I knew the best thing to do was to find a quiet spot to still my thoughts and wait for God to reassure me with His peace. I quietly counselled myself to be strong and not become defeated, excusing myself early in the evening to go to bed. I knew they all meant well and were concerned at all the difficulties and setbacks I was experiencing, but it was just adding more pressure to the already difficult situation. I had never travelled overseas before, so I had to trust God to lead and protect us and open the right doors for us as we kept to the original plans. Backing out now was not an option! On Sunday morning, I got a call from my buddy Gillian, who was studying at YWAM in Auckland. She wanted to visit me, which cheered me up immediately as Gillian had a wonderful sense of humour and was very supportive of what I was doing. She came with us to a busy market, then returned to Margy and Fred's for the evening meal. Soon after, Bev and Ian arrived with the last few boxes to be stored at Margy's. These would be sent on to us at a later date.

We had located an airfreight company that only charged six dollars a kilo instead of twelve which was a significant saving. Bev, Gillian and I spent time in the van praying for peace for my family and me during these last few days. We took authority over the anxiety and panic that had crept in. It felt wonderful to be with my special friends at this time. Gillian and I sang our favourite worship songs as she drove me back to Margy's.

Later that evening as Sophie and I prepared beds for the children upstairs, we were aware that a special season of living in the same town and being able to visit each other regularly was now over. I had no idea when we would be able to return to New Zealand again. It was a lot to process emotionally for us both.

For several weeks I had been waiting for news from the South African embassy in Sydney about the return of our passports. Finally, I heard from Denise, the agent, who asked me what I wanted to do now that we knew the entry and study visas had all been denied. The embassy had sent all our paperwork and documents to South Africa long ago and had been waiting for a reply from them but they hadn't received an explanation as to why the visas were all denied. I instructed Denise to return the passports to us immediately as we only had three days left before we flew to Australia. We would be stopping over in Sydney, London, and Nairobi before reaching Capetown in South Africa. As a novice traveller, the itinerary I had chosen looked exciting and adventurous to me.

The sobering reality now was that we were about to embark on this long journey that spanned three continents without the necessary paperwork to disembark at our final destination, Capetown. Denise was concerned for us and suggested I visit the embassy in Sydney. She was apologetic and also perplexed as to why the visas hadn't been granted. I thanked her for all her help and said goodbye, with no idea how the situation was going to be resolved. I was determined to trust God and let Him guide us in the midst of this. There was nothing further I could do about the visas now, so I just needed to focus on our final days and see what happened once we reached Sydney.

On Saturday, we cleaned up quickly after breakfast so we could enjoy a day out at a local beach. I enjoyed being able to spoil Sophie and the girls by buying them clothes at the shopping emporium and then had fun splashing in the water with my two little nieces as we paddled in the shallow waters. That evening was our Christmas celebration. We ate wonderful food and began handing out gifts to each other. As the music played in the background, we all enjoyed the warm, loving family atmosphere. We hugged and murmured words of appreciation to each other while exchanging gifts. Generous Margy gave me $800. Her concern for us and all the practical support over the years had made a huge difference to our lives. My family are all generous and compassionate people for whom I am truly grateful.

I spent the next day writing letters to friends and inserting a prayer card with our photo on, asking them to keep us in their thoughts and prayers. Our bank details were at the bottom of the card. Hopefully, some would decide to begin supporting us financially once we began missions training. Asking friends for finance was not something I had done before so I felt uncomfortable with this aspect of our new life. Without the guidance of experienced missionaries, I wasn't sure how to approach this sensitive but vital topic. As it was for Hudson Taylor, who had gone to China as a missionary 100 years ago, I was hoping that my testimony would be, "Where God guides, He provides."

Once again I was up very late sewing a garment for my niece Mandy. Sophie stayed up to keep me company, which I appreciated as I was no longer feeling very motivated. The day that we were to leave New Zealand was almost here.

Monday morning I was wide awake at 5 a.m.. We had breakfast and packed the cars with all the luggage. Sophie's young daughter announced that she wanted to stay the night with me in Africa and then go back home to her family. We laughed at her childlike concept of the situation. Margy and Fred drove the lads and me to the airport, while Mum, Sophie, and her family followed us in their car.

After checking in our luggage and receiving our boarding passes, I turned to hug my family goodbye. Sophie had been crying all weekend on and off, which made me teary as well. What do you say to your Mum and family when you have no idea when you will see them again? It was a sobering moment, and yet I was anxious to get onto the plane so I could finally switch off all the decision-making. I joked with the family about flying around the world until we were asked to leave the plane. "They will have to put us down somewhere in the world," I declared.

After hugs and farewells, the lads and I headed for immigration and the departure lounge. I bought a camera for Eli at the duty-free shop so he could take photos of his family when he arrived in Zimbabwe. I originally had no idea how to take money for the trip, but Bev, who has travelled overseas before, informed me that traveller's cheques were the safest way to carry a large sum of money. Being practical, she had arranged this for me before we left Coniston. At the airport, I changed some notes for Australian dollars so we would have cash when we landed.

The boys and I boarded our flight, each deep in thought. I knew Josh was unhappy about leaving his friends and family; he wanted to stay in New Zealand. Eli, who doesn't like change, was being uprooted and about to embark on a long journey by himself to Zimbabwe. Once we landed in Sydney, he would catch a flight to South Africa, then another one to Zimbabwe where he would meet his father and his family. It was a huge step into the unknown, which had seemed exciting when he was talking to his dad on the phone about it, but which might prove quite overwhelming and lonely once he said goodbye to us in Sydney.

I savoured the sensation of finally taking an international trip after so many years of longing to travel abroad, regularly praying, "Father, please let me go overseas, even if it's just to Australia." Many young people in New Zealand travel overseas once they leave school. I once read in a magazine that at any given time, around 20% of people under age 25 in New Zealand are travelling abroad. We are a curious and adventurous nation.

After stowing our hand luggage in the overhead compartments, the three of us settled into our seats and prepared for the biggest adventure of our lives.

Looking Back

In the years ahead, I learned that it is common to encounter many obstacles as you set out on a faith journey with God. The enemy does his best to discourage and derail the plans of those who set their heart on obeying the calling of God.

Because of this, forgiveness needs to become a lifestyle and not an occasional event. All of us hurt and disappoint people without meaning to because we often have issues we've not dealt with that impact and hinder our relationships. I am grateful to all the spiritual leaders that I had in New Zealand who did their best to guide and care for me. I am grateful to God that those who were trying to be protective and didn't understand the calling to Africa were able to understand in the years ahead that God had indeed called me to this mission field. Despite the fact that my decisions probably looked reckless to my family, they loved and supported us in wonderful ways. Even though I was a young, single mother with two children, it was His plan for us to leave everything and everyone we knew and follow Him to an unknown continent. Over time, I was able to reconcile with those who had not understood and also to apologise where I had become critical. Keeping an uncluttered heart is so important in order to be able to hear God's voice clearly.

The truth is that we are all a work in progress on the potter's wheel. He alone knows the shape and design of the vessel He is busy producing.

The End.

My faithful friend Viv Fisk borrowed a van to drive us to Auckland two weeks before we flew out

The boys and I at my sister's place, contemplating leaving our family, not knowing when we would see them again

My brave little family at the airport, about to venture out into the vast unknown

This is the official photo that Bev took for our support cards. We are doing our best to look confident and happy

References

Carothers, Merlin R. *Power in Praise*.
Eastbourne: Kingsway Publications, 1974.

Cunningham, Loren. *Is That Really You, God?*
[Place of Publication Not Identified]: Baker Book House, 1984.

Renich, Fred. *When the Chisel Hits the Rock*.
Wheaton, IL: Victor Books, 1980.

Acknowledgements

My heartfelt thanks and gratitude to all those who have helped me with the various aspects of creating my first book. We did it!

A big thank you to my generous, caring, supportive sons Joshua and Eli, and my lovely daughter-in-laws, for your encouragement and belief in my dream to write about my life story –an abundance of incredible adventures, which seemed quite crazy and reckless at times!

To Vimbayi for suggesting the great title and to Becks for the website.

To my sisters Avian Mcmanus and Sylvie Forester and close friend Ruth Robertson who gave me honest feedback after reading the final draft.

To Colleen Doyle for her generous affirmation and encouragement and for writing the forward. Your life is an enormous inspiration to so many.

To my wonderful, generous friends Laura Spargo and Kay Solomon for dedicating many hours proof reading and helping me to make some hard decisions as we shaped the story.

To content editor and friend Natalie Techentin (USA) for her sharp editing skills, helpful advice, patience, flexibility and encouragement.

To Rob and Lyn Packer – for walking me through the process of self-publishing and honest feedback for a tricky chapter.

Carmen Lye – an incredibly creative graphic designer and journalist who has become a valued friend, for the beautiful cover design, the layout and doing all that was necessary to get the final draft ready for printing. I am so grateful for all your many talents and your commitment to helping this book become a reality.

And finally, to all the many friends who over the past 30 years have said "Chris, you must write these amazing stories." Thank you for your belief in my ability to do so and know that you each played a special part in this book becoming a reality.

Enjoy this first book –I am already busy with the next one:

Courage in the Cape

Which follows Christine and the boys as they arrive in South Africa during the end of the Apartheid regime; just before Nelson Mandela is released from the infamous Robben Island.

Then, as the boys settle into new schools, Christine begins her missionary training with Youth With A Mission, and all three of them struggle as they encounter and adjust to several new cultures.

Ignoring local people's advice to not to go into 'coloured or African' townships alone (as it can be dangerous), she knocks on people's doors and introduces herself to many shocked residents who have never had a white person visit their home during their lifetime. By doing this, she hears the stories of suffering and tenacity and feels the heartbeat of some of the disadvantaged groups who will later become the focus of her ministry.

Marvel at how God provides for this little family who knew nothing about raising support before leaving New Zealand and thus have to rely on God daily for all their basic needs.

Learn some key lessons with Christine as God teaches her to overcome fear of man and anxiety, to gain confidence in His guidance and to bring compassion and dignity to those in great need around her.

Contact :

If this book has impacted or inspired you, please email Christine as she would love to hear from you:

Email: chris@courageseries.com

Website: courageseries.com

Take a look at Christine's testimony on fantailstudios.com